Twayne's Theatrical Arts Series

Warren French
EDITOR

Mike Nichols

Mike Nichols

Mike Nichols

H. WAYNE SCHUTH

University of New Orleans

BOSTON

Twayne Publishers

1978

Mike Nichols

is first published in 1978 by Twayne Publishers,
A Division of G. K. Hall & Co.

Copyright © 1978 by G. K. Hall & Co.

Printed on permanent/durable acid-free paper and bound in the
United States of America

First Printing, May 1978

Library of Congress Cataloging in Publication Data

Schuth, H. Wayne.
Mike Nichols.

(Twayne's theatrical arts series)
"Filmography": p. 171–74.
Bibliography: p. 165–70.
Includes index.
1. Nichols, Mike.
PN1998.A3N487   791.43'0233'0924   77-26744
ISBN 0-8057-9255-4

Contents

About the Author

Editor's Foreword

Preface

Chronology

1. The Artist   19

2. *Who's Afraid of Virginia Woolf?*   27

3. *The Graduate*   45

4. *Catch-22*   65

5. *Carnal Knowledge*   85

6. *The Day of the Dolphin*   111

7. *The Fortune*   129

8. "Family"   145

9. The Nichols Touch   151

    Notes and References   161

    Selected Bibliography   165

    Filmography   171

    Index   175

About the Author

H. Wayne Schuth was born in Oak Park, Illinois, on May 25, 1942, and grew up in Chicago. He received a Bachelor of Science degree with a major in Radio, Television, and Film, and a Master of Arts degree in Radio, Television, and Film from Northwestern University in Evanston, Illinois. He received a Doctor of Philosophy degree with a major in Film and Communications from The Ohio State University in Columbus, Ohio. He has worked in production at commercial television studios in Chicago. He taught film and television at Stephens College in Columbia, Missouri, The Ohio State University in Columbus, Ohio, and is currently teaching at The University of New Orleans in New Orleans, Louisiana. He has directed nine non-theatrical films which are widely distributed, including *Are Poets People?* which won an Eagle Certificate from the Council on International Non-Theatrical Events. He was a film critic on station WOSU-TV in Columbus, Ohio, where he showed films and analyzed them. He has published numerous articles on film in scholarly journals and in film books. He was editor of the *Digest of the University Film Association* and Executive Vice-President of the Association for two years. He is a member of the Advisory Council of the University Film Foundation.

Editor's Foreword

Mike Nichols has had a most unusual career as a film director. Few other directors have appeared so suddenly in such a conspicuous position. Most have served long apprenticeships in various capacities before they have been entrusted with a major production. Nichols, however, came directly from working as an actor and theatrical director to assume responsibility for the film version of Edward Albee's highly successful and controversial play, *Who's Afraid of Virginia Woolf?*, starring Elizabeth Taylor and Richard Burton, two of the screen's most highly paid and highly publicized stars.

Despite the additional burden of having to face down threats of censorship to the then-daring screenplay, Nichols with this single picture established himself as a major film celebrity. The film proved in every way a match for the celebrated play upon which it is based, and it has become a motion picture classic, one of the last great emotional dramas to be filmed in traditional black and white.

With his next picture, however, Nichols proved himself a master of color effects and scored an even greater personal triumph with *The Graduate*. Few American pictures have enjoyed such immediate critical and personal success. Young audiences—feeling that the film told their own story of frustration and rebellion against a plastic society—thronged theaters, and Nichols won the Academy Award as the best director of the year. With just two films, he had won a place in the very top rank of film directors and had created what may be called "the picture of its generation"—as *The Birth of a Nation* and *The Grapes of Wrath* had been of earlier generations.

Nichols has not continued, however, to enjoy such unvarying success. His third picture, *Catch-22*, based on Joseph Heller's best-selling anti-war fantasy, was not universally well received, although the author of the novel liked it. Filming *Catch-22* posed several problems. First, the novel itself had had a mixed reception because of its seemingly shapeless structure. Also probably everyone who did admire Heller's satire had his own ideas about how a film version should be cast and plotted. Most important, no one at the time of the release of the film seems to have appreciated the complex and appropriate dream structure that Nichols and scenarist Buck Henry imposed upon Heller's sprawling work. One of the great values of Wayne Schuth's book is that his perceptive analysis of the intricate design of this film should lead to its revaluation as a work of art.

Nichols' fourth film, *Carnal Knowledge*, is perhaps his most personal statement. It was not, like his three earlier films, derived from another medium, but rather was written especially for the screen by the vitriolic cartoonist/playwright Jules Feiffer; and it is an even more mordant attack on the loneliness and lovelessness of the sexually oriented life than *Virginia Woolf* and *The Graduate* were. Perhaps because of the subject matter—explicitly suggested by the title—and the memorable portrayals of young neurotics by Jack Nicholson, Arthur Garfunkel, Candice Bergen, and Ann-Margret, the film was critically and commercially successful, though its reception only palely shadowed that of *The Graduate*.

As Wayne Schuth points out, Nichols begins to move in this film toward adapting to the screen the stripped-down design and simplified colors of abstract painting. The experiment was artistically strikingly successful; and, as Schuth observes, "*Carnal Knowledge* is a beautiful film to watch with the soundtrack turned off because of the visual design elements." But Nichols may have been getting too far ahead of his audience. One of the most sophisticated persons ever to direct commercial films, Nichols permeated *Carnal Knowledge* and the succeeding *The Day of the Dolphin* with a kind of elegant, Modernist despair that probably disturbed audiences who still go to the movies primarily to be entertained—shocked and titillated perhaps, but finally reassured.

There is no reassurance to be found in Nichols' last film to date, *The Fortune*, a sardonic tale of two wastrels plotting to murder a rich girl during the garish 1920s. The picture is in the same vein as Chaplin's *Monsieur Verdoux*. Though that is probably Chaplin's most carefully plotted and stylistically consistent film, it has never been popular with general audiences because of the slapstick treatment of morbid subject matter. The lack of enthusiasm for *The Fortune* indicates that Nichols had lost the audience he had won with *The Graduate* by making too many demands on their generally sentimental sensibilities.

Through this meteoric rise and subsequent slowdown there has been no doubt, however, about Nichols' relationship to the films that he signs. He is not simply, as François Truffaut puts it, the man who provides the pictures; rather he carefully designs every element of his productions to achieve a carefully calculated effect. Wayne Schuth points out that Nichols told a *Playboy* interviewer, "I have to have final authority—not because I'm so terrific but because the picture has to be informed by *one* vision." "Informed by *one* vision"—never has the *auteurist* concept of artistic creation been more succinctly summed up! Perhaps the thing that will surprise readers of this book most is its revelation of how extremely self-conscious Nichols has been of the contribution of every detail to the success of his films.

Since filming *The Fortune*, Mike Nichols has been preoccupied with successful theatrical projects. If he does not return to the screen, this book will serve as a record of one remarkable episode in the artistic development of the film; for Nichols has been—with Robert Altman and Michelangelo Antonioni (to whom Schuth often refers)—a leader in bringing belatedly to the screen the alienated Modernist sensibility that has dominated twentieth-century writing in the United States and Europe. If he does return—as I speculate he will—this account of the remarkable first phase of his career will enable us to see it in perspective against his later achievements, for perhaps Nichols will return to film, newly attuned to a new audience. Centainly he has shown his capacity to move with the times in his enormously successful theatrical production of *Annie*.

WARREN FRENCH

Preface

Mike Nichols is a great filmmaker who has had an impact on contemporary filmmaking and who deals eloquently with the human condition, offering images that may help people make sense out of troubling and difficult events.

In this book, I analyze how Nichols articulates ideas through the complex symbol system of film and I explore the consistent themes and elements of style in his work. I relate his films to an audience that responds, and continues to respond, to his vision. I evaluate his significance to the development of the motion picture.

Nichols' style is consistent, and similar themes and concerns can be found in all his films. He seems to be making the same film over and over again, whether it be the nonchronological *Catch-22*, the episodic *Carnal Knowledge*, or the narrative *The Day of the Dolphin*. He is characteristic of what the French call the film *auteur*. He is in complete control of his work and places on it his signature or the stamp of his personality. Although he uses plays or novels as raw material for some of his films, each film has the Nichols touch and each can be seen as a part of a coherent, profound vision of the human condition by a major artist.

As I analyze Nichols' films, I will show how important what he calls "the spine" is to the brilliance of his work. Although Nichols enjoys collaboration and likes working with others and sharing ideas, his is the final guiding vision.

In his famous skits with Elaine May and in his films, Nichols deals with most serious situations, but often deals with those situations through laughter. His comic moments appeal to the intellect, and through the laughter, incongruities and often the truth underlying those incongruities can be clearly seen.

Before discussing Mike Nichols' use of film I will explain some of my basic assumptions about film as a symbolic device.

Film is a complex symbol system, made up of images, words, and sounds. All three can be used symbolically. Within an image, for example, camera distance, angle, and placement may be used intentionally to communicate what the director wishes and so create a meaning, or they may unintentionally communicate something. They may not even have any meaning related to the film as a whole. A color or a costume may work the same way. Nichols, I feel, wishes all the elements of the symbol system to communicate his vision intentionally, and it will be pointed out that he feels it is necessary to relate his symbols to the spine of his work.

Words are symbols, and sounds too can have symbolic meaning; but it is extremely significant that images can function as symbols.

On the most obvious level, film images can be viewed as a series of signs for various realities. Edgar Dale in *Audio-Visual Methods in Teaching* calls images semi-symbolic signs. He proposes a continuum where images can re-present the real world, or represent abstractions symbolically. For example, suppose we have an image of the capitol building in Washington, D.C. The sign level of the image is a re-presenting of the building. The symbolic level of the building may represent patriotism, America, love of country, and the like. Images can fall on the continuum on the sign level, the symbol level, or somewhere in between. Another way of looking at it is to discuss a symbol's denotative and connotative meaning. In a Nichols' film, the color of a wall may be white. On the denotative level, white is just the color of the wall. It re-presents the reality. On the connotative level, Nichols may mean it to stand for a cool, sterile environment. It represents sterility.

As I analyze the films of Mike Nichols, I will rely heavily on this distinction between sign and symbol and between the denotative and the connotative use of the film medium.

One should be aware that the films of Mike Nichols may now be seen in three forms. The first is the form in which the films were first intended to be shown in theaters, uncut and in an anamorphic, widescreen format if originally released that way. The second is the way the films are shown on television. In these versions, some scenes, shots, or words may be shortened or deleted for censorship reasons (when *The Day of the Dolphin* was shown on television, part of the shot where someone said . . . "one *hell* of a dolphin hunt" was out) or time reasons. Anamorphic widescreen pictures may be cropped to accommodate the aspect ratio of the small television screen. The cropping will often show just part of a scene. For example, if two characters are sitting in a room talking, in the original anamorphic version, you would see both characters. In the cropped television version, you may see first one character and then the other character. Cuts, or simultaneous transitions within the shot, will have been added. In some cases, there will be a pan or horizontal movement from one character to another which is added in making the television version. These changes are made by a technical process from the original anamorphic version. The third form is very much like the television form. It is a cropped "flat" print made from an anamorphic original to be shown in film societies and universities which do not have anamorphic lenses. All Nichols' feature films except *Who's Afraid of Virginia Woolf?* were shot in the anamorphic widescreen format. The analyses of the films in this book were all done with the prints that were intended for showing in theaters as they were first released, and except for *Who's Afraid of Virginia Woolf?* in the original anamorphic widescreen process. "Family," a television series also analyzed, is shot in the standard non-anamorphic format for television release.

I wish to thank those who have made this book possible. Special thanks go to Twayne Series Editor Warren French for his help, encouragement, brilliant insights, and editing. Also thanks to George Zulandt of The Ohio State University, Mansfield, who read and edited the first draft of the manuscript.

Many thanks go, too, to The University of New Orleans Graduate Research Council and The University of New Orleans College of Liberal Arts Research Committee for grants to help with this book. I also wish to thank Lane Bonham and Ralph Hogan of The University of New Orleans Audio-Visual Center; Cooper R. Mackin, Dean of the College of Liberal Arts; W. Harlan Shaw, Chairman of the Department of Drama and Communications; and Carolyn Kay of the University Center Program. Special thanks also go to my research assistants Stephanie Samuel and George Tubbs, University of New Orleans students John Craven, Ginny Jones, Cindee Shaffer, Frank Walsh, and the many other students at The University of New Orleans who made my work during this study so enjoyable.

Thanks go to Kathleen Caruso who typed the final manuscript; Hal Sherman of 20th Century-Fox; Paul Simon for permission to use certain lyrics from his songs; Lori Surdaki of Swank Motion Pictures; and Warner Brothers for stills from *Who's Afraid of Virginia Woolf?*

Thanks also to the many other people who helped me in various ways with the book, including David Cuthbert, Martin Maloney, Suzanne Ormond, John Ormond, Samuel E. Rubin, M.D., Win Sharples, Jr., August W. Staub, and Robert W. Wagner.

Finally, my wife, Mary Schuth, and my son, Andrew Schuth, deserve much credit for their understanding, patience, kindness, and sense of humor, without which the work would have been much more difficult.

Chronology

1931   Mike Nichols born Michael Igor Peschkowsky in Berlin, Germany, November 6.

1939   Comes to United States.

1944   Becomes United States citizen.

1950– Attends University of Chicago.
1953

1954   Meets Elaine May.

1955   Studies with Lee Strasberg in New York; joins Compass Players.

1957   Nichols and May appear on "The Jack Paar Show."

1960   Opens on Broadway in *An Evening with Mike Nichols and Elaine May*, October 8.

1961   Closes in *An Evening with Mike Nichols and Elaine May*, July 1; the team of Nichols and May disbands.

1963   Directs the play *Barefoot in the Park* on Broadway.

1964   Directs the play *The Knack* off-Broadway and the play *Luv* on Broadway.

1965   Directs the play *The Odd Couple* on Broadway.

1966   Directs the play *The Apple Tree* on Broadway and the film *Who's Afraid of Virginia Woolf?*

1967   Directs the play *The Little Foxes* on Broadway and the film *The Graduate*. Receives Academy Award for Best Director, *The Graduate*.

1968   Directs the play *Plaza Suite* on Broadway.

1970   Directs the film *Catch-22*.

1971   Directs the play *The Prisoner of Second Avenue* on Broadway and the film *Carnal Knowledge*.

1973   Directs the play *Uncle Vanya* on Broadway and the film *The Day of the Dolphin*.

1975   Directs the film *The Fortune*.

1976   Directs the plays *Streamers* and *Comedians* on Broadway. Produces the television series "Family."

1977   Presents the play *Annie* on Broadway. Directs the play *The Gin Game* on Broadway.

Nichols is married to Annabel and has two children, Max and Jenny. He has another daughter, Daisy, by a previous marriage.

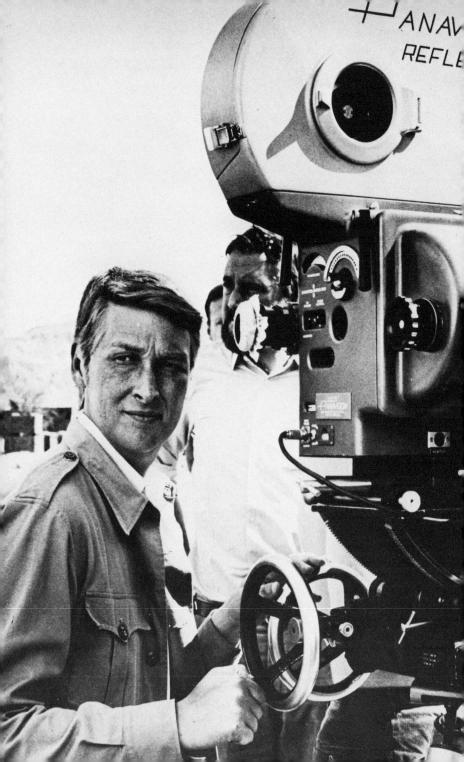

1

The Artist

ON NOVEMBER 6, 1931, Mike Nichols was born Michael Igor Peschkowsky, to a Jewish family in Berlin. His father was Paul Peschkowsky, a doctor who had been born in Russia and moved to Germany after the Revolution. His mother was Brigitte Landauer. His maternal grandparents were Hedwig Lachmann, who provided Richard Strauss with the German libretto of *Salome* and Gustav Landauer, head of German Social Democrat Party, who was later executed by the Nazis. Hitler became Chancellor when Michael was two years old. Michael can remember going to a segregated school for Jewish children and being harassed by the non-Jewish children.

With the situation becoming more and more oppressive in Germany, Michael's father came to America in 1938, changed his name to Paul Nichols, took his medical exam, and set up practice in Manhattan. A year later he sent for his family. Only Michael and his older brother were able to come as their mother was ill. She came in 1941, a few weeks before the United States entered the war.

Dr. Nichols was successful and maintained his family well in the West Seventies, near Central Park. He died in 1944 of leukemia. Michael attended Cherry Lane School in Darien, Connecticut, the Dalton School, and the Walden High School in New York. He does not feel he learned very much at any of them. He remembers them as a series of "very chic, very progressive schools, where we were taught French from playing cards and were served something every hour—second breakfast, mid-morning snack, hearty lunch, early afternoon cookies."[1]

Nichols was lonely and had few friends. At fourteen he became stagestruck, but the dramatics teacher at Cherry Lane School told him that although intelligent, he was not suited for the stage. He graduated from Walden and then registered at New York University. He soon dropped out and took a job as a shipping clerk in a

19

company that made costume jewelery. Seeing little future in this, he decided on an academic course and enrolled in the pre-medical program at the University of Chicago. He aimed at becoming a psychiatrist.

"I thought I could cut classes and still pass," said Nichols, who was able to do just that.[2] He supported himself with a variety of odd jobs. He became more and more interested in theater and joined many theater groups. During a performance of Strindberg's *Miss Julie*, he first became aware of Elaine May, who was to play such an important role in his future work. As Nichols performed on the stage, he saw the dark-haired coed "staring cruelly from the audience through the whole thing."[3] The next day, as he was reading his rave reviews, Ms. May came up behind him, read the reviews over his shoulder, and said in a sneering tone, "Ha." Nichols says he ignored her. Ms. May says he wept. In any case, he avoided becoming acquainted with her because he was sure she regarded him with contempt. Ms. May denies that she ever regarded Nichols with contempt. "I didn't regard him at all," she says.

They finally began speaking to each other one spring evening in 1954. Nichols was on his way home from his announcing job at a local radio station. He was walking through the waiting room of the Illinois Central Station at Randolph Street in Chicago, and he saw Ms. May reading a magazine on a bench. He sat down next to her and assumed the role of a secret agent contacting a fellow spy. She answered in a heavy Russian accent, and they did the first Nichols-May improvisation.[4]

They were yet to develop these improvisations in any professional way for some time. About six months after their meeting at the station, Nichols decided to study acting with Lee Strasberg at the Actor's Studio in New York. He again supported himself with various odd jobs. One of them was waiting tables in a Howard Johnson's restaurant. It ended the night a customer asked him what kind of ice cream he would recommend for a hot fudge sundae. The tired Nichols replied, "How about chicken?"[5] He taught horseback riding, which may have led to something he enjoys very much today, the breeding and selling of Arabian horses. He finally took a job as a radio station announcer in Philadelphia and commuted to New York for his acting lessons.

In Chicago, Elaine May joined one of the theater companies Nichols had been in. In the spring of 1955, the Fire Department closed the company's theater, and David Shepherd, a theater buff, organized the Compass Theatre. The Compass was like a nightclub where performers improvised scenes based on ideas they thought up or elicited from the audience. The Compass Players included Ms. May and then such unknown artists as Alan Arkin, Shelley Berman, Barbara Harris, Zorah Lampert, and Nichols himself, who was asked by Shepherd to come from Philadelphia to fill a vacancy. Many of the routines that made Nichols and May famous were developed at the Compass.

In the fall of 1957, because of a complex of business ailments, the Compass was disbanded in Chicago and a new Compass started in St. Louis with Nichols and May. It lasted four months. There were hopes of taking the Compass to New York, but this did not work out. Nichols had gotten the name of New York manager Jack Rollins from a friend. Rollins was looking for new acts to manage. When Nichols and May were in New York, negotiating for the Compass to come there, they had lunch with Rollins. He was very impressed with them as they did sketches for him at the table. He arranged for a more formal interview later, and then decided to represent them. He arranged for them to audition at the Blue Angel and the club's owner immediately offered them a booking.[6] The team soon became a favorite and repeated their success in other American cities. Nichols and May made their television debut on the Jack Paar Show in 1957 during their Blue Angel engagement and soon appeared on other television shows, including "Omnibus," "The Steve Allen Show," and the "Fabulous Fifties." Nichols even had a dramatic role on the "Playhouse 90" production of Roger O. Hirson's *Journey to the Day*, in which he played a manic-depressive actor.

On May 1, 1959, there was a concert presentation of Nichols and May at New York's Town Hall, and on October 8, 1960, *An Evening with Mike Nichols and Elaine May* opened on Broadway at the John Golden Theatre with a cast of two.

During the successful run, Nichols and May, in addition to appearing on television programs, were involved in other activities. They did the voices for a series of animated commercials for Jax Beer, a local New Orleans brand, that are still well remembered in New Orleans. The names of the performers were never mentioned. Nichols and May taped a series of one- to five-minute improvised comedy spots which were inserted, at the rate of five times a weekend, into NBC's weekend program "Monitor." They recorded five record albums.

On July 1, 1961, *An Evening with Mike Nichols and Elaine May*

closed on Broadway, and the team disbanded. Nichols wanted to
direct (his first directing was a production of Yeats' *Purgatory* while
at the University of Chicago), so he went to Vancouver, Canada,
where he directed *The Importance of Being Ernest* and acted the
Dauphin in Shaw's *St. Joan.*[7]

In the Nichols and May skits, there are foreshadowings of thematic and stylistic elements that appear in his films. All of them—like
Nichols' films—deal almost exclusively with people from the upper
middle class. Although the skits are very funny, they also concern
themselves with a difficult universe, where there is much hurt,
selfishness, and cruelty. It may be funny when a domineering
mother makes her son feel so guilty about not calling her that it
reduces him to infantilism, but there is also a real horror in the
situation. The same may be said of a poor fellow trying to make a
phone call and confronting inhuman telephone operators, a patient
who torments his psychiatrist when he tells her the reasons behind
not attending a session, a doctor who refuses to sew up a patient
until a nurse agrees to have a relationship with him, or a doctor who
is more concerned about a nurse asking about him than a patient's
health. Robert Rice, writing in *The New Yorker*, comments on one
skit, "Pirandello": "It lets them express in detail what is conceivably
a chief ingredient of their common view of life—that people,
whether they are children, adults, actors, or Nichols and May, treat
each other the same way—abominably."[8] When discussing his play
Streamers and his film *The Fortune,* Nichols said, "There's no good
play or story in which some things aren't funny, even the most
serious ones—It seems to me that if the moment is legitimate and
truthful, then the audience should be free to react in any way they
want."[9]

In several Nichols and May skits, there are patterns that later
appear in the films. In the skits, for example, are many domineering, often destructive women. In "Telephone," domineering
women telephone operators reduce the male caller to tears.[10] In
"Mother and Son," a domineering mother manipulates her son's
guilt feelings. The domineering, often destructive woman appears
in one form or another in the six Nichols feature films analyzed in
this book. Another pattern in the skits involves two men having sex
with the same woman. In "Adultery," a man and woman discuss the
woman's husband with great affection and respect. In "A Little
More Gauze," a doctor accuses a nurse of betraying him with

another man. In "Second Piano Concerto," a dentist is in love with his married patient (a take-off on the British film *Brief Encounter*). In the skit "Bach to Bach," one character remarks that there are no absolutes in a relationship. This theme will also be found in Nichols' films. Other themes in the skits that will recur in Nichols' films are the influence of the past upon the present and the separation of sex from love. All the elements work together to form a coherent, artistic, and profound unity both in each film considered separately and in all the films considered as a single *oeuvre*. This unity is the vision of Mike Nichols.

Before beginning to make films, however, Nichols enhanced his reputation as a stage director. In 1963, producer Saint Subber asked him to direct *Barefoot in the Park* by Neil Simon, first at the Bucks County Playhouse in Pennsylvania and then on Broadway.[11] The show was a hit, and Nichols won a Tony award for best director. In 1964, Nichols directed *The Knack*, a four-character British comedy for off-Broadway's Establishment Theatre Company. It introduced George Segal, who was later to play Nick in the four-character Nichols film, *Who's Afraid of Virginia Woolf?* Also in 1964, Nichols directed the National Company of *Barefoot in the Park*, as well as Murray Schisgal's *Luv* on Broadway. All were successes, and *Luv* also won him a Tony award for best director.

In 1965, he directed Neil Simon's *The Odd Couple* and won a Tony award for best director. In 1966, he was offered the chance to direct the film *The Graduate*, but he waited until he had directed *Who's Afraid of Virginia Woolf?* as a special favor to Elizabeth Taylor and Richard Burton. He also directed the stage musical *The Apple Tree* that year. *The Apple Tree* is a trio of stories, one of which was written by Jules Feiffer, who was later to write the screenplay for Nichols' film *Carnal Knowledge*.

Nichols is regarded in theater and film as a fine director and has won many awards for his work. His successful directing has been referred to as "the Nichols touch." I shall analyze that touch. His work in film has many comic moments as well as a deep, profound, and disturbing vision of the human condition. He has a consistent style, and everything in his films seems there for a reason.

In referring to his style, Nichols has said, "The thing about something that's made right—whether it's a novel, or an opera, or a film—has to do with being hung on a spine. Why do composers go to all the trouble of inverting what they did in the first act? Or basing, let's say, the score of *West Side Story* on five notes? And each song is a variation of this theme that Bernstein had in his head. Why is it useful? I think because the stronger the spine, the stronger the backbone of the thing that you're making, the more—whether openly or secretly—everything that happens is tied into that backbone. The more solid it is, maybe the truer it is. When you work on a play you discover that every choice you make, every costume, every radiator on the set, the placement of everything, has to do with the spine that you've chosen."[12]

Nichols has said, "There is no democracy in this kind of work. I have to have final authority—not because I'm so terrific but because the picture has to be informed by *one* vision. Right is might, but whether I'm right or wrong, it all has to be built around one central idea."[13]

The sense of collaboration can be seen in his early work with the Compass Theatre where the improvisation certainly depended on team work.

Nichols also enjoys the repartee between two characters that he developed so brilliantly in his skits with Elaine May. Jan Dawson, writing on *The Graduate* in *Sight and Sound* remarks, "Nichols' second feature inevitably reminds one of those brilliant gramaphone records on which he and Elaine May, in a series of four or five minute dialogues, worked their way through a succession of characterizations and situations—two Feifferish characters, never so distorted to be unrecognizable, each of them determined to have the last word."[14] Dawson is right, for Nichols does extremely well when he has two characters talk to each other. This can be found in all his films, as will be illustrated later, and in *Carnal Knowledge*, Feiffer himself does the script.

In my analysis, Nichols' films will be looked at not just in this frame of reference, however, but in many, in the belief that there is no one universal frame that applies to all films. Different ones are useful for different films, and they grow out of the films themselves. The frames of reference are ways of discovering meanings in the works. Semiology, psychology, mythology, and the like are useful frames of reference, but no one method is all-encompassing and correct. And so, many frames of reference are used here to analyze Nichols' films coherently. Also, it is important to keep in mind that the analysis here is my *interpretation* of Nichols' films.

Mike Nichols raises important issues with his films. He entertains us. He makes us laugh, cry, think, and feel. His films are extremely relevant to the contemporary human condition. I shall analyze in depth both the form and the content of these brilliant films.

2

Who's Afraid of Virginia Woolf?

Who's Afraid of Virginia Woolf? was Mike Nichols' first film. He was scheduled to direct *The Graduate* for producer Lawrence Turman, but at the request of the Burtons, Turman allowed Nichols to make *Who's Afraid of Virginia Woolf?* first.

Originally written as a play by Edward Albee and adapted for the screen by Ernest Lehman and Nichols, the movie concerns George, an associate professor of History (Richard Burton) and his college-educated wife, Martha (Elizabeth Taylor), both in their forties. Her father is president of the college. After one of her father's parties, Martha invites a new faculty couple over for drinks. The newcomers are Nick (George Segal), a young member of the Biology Department, and his wife, Honey (Sandy Dennis). The four spend the night in what Albee named the acts in his play: "Fun and Games," "Walpurgisnacht," and "Exorcism."[1] During the conversation and arguments, souls are stripped bare and each character comes to new insight and understanding.

Through visual imagery, Nichols prepares us for the death and rebirth of the characters. At the beginning of the film, George and Martha are walking home from the party. As they walk across the campus, dead leaves are blowing in the wind. This autumn atmosphere suggests the end of a cycle, as one approaches the cold winter or death.

Nichols also uses a full moon on this Saturday night. This may equate with the Walpurgisnacht, or time of demons, before they are exorcised on All Saints Day. At the conclusion of the film, it is dawn on Sunday, after the exorcism.

In the first scene of the film, George and Martha are walking through the campus to their home after the party. George tries to quiet Martha's loud laughter, and she calls him a "cluck." Later, she reveals to Honey and Nick how disgusted she is by her husband and

27

his lack of ambition. George retaliates verbally. George and Martha constantly bicker over a son who is no longer living with them; as it turns out later, the child is purely imaginary. George and Martha attack each other throughout the film until George, finally driven to desperation, kills his and Martha's mythical son, an act that finally shatters Martha. The son is an interesting symbol; Nichols describes it as a metaphor for a couple of things: "One is for what exists between people when they love each other and what they build between each other . . . Then it also appears to be connected with George and Martha's hangup . . . the need to attack what is good."[2]

So the son binds George and Martha together, and by "killing" their son, George has performed the ultimate act of one-upmanship. He is a manipulator to the extreme. He bases his decisions on their effects over others and is very control-oriented, although we often feel that he is pushed into his retaliations.

In the play, George and Martha are given equal attention. But in the film, George is the pivotal character. It is actually his film. The camera stays with him most of the time and we see things primarily from his point of view. It is George who sees the car parked on the lawn and the shadows of Martha and Nick in the upstairs window. It is George who finally strikes the crucial blow against Martha. The film concentrates on George's lack of success. According to Martha, he is "a bog in the History Department." He came to the college when he was quite young and married the president's daughter. However, her father saw more and more that he was not the one to become Chairman of the History Department or eventually to succeed him as president. George tried to publish an autobiographical novel, but when the president ordered him not to publish it, he submitted.

In this novel, a boy accidentally killed his mother with a shotgun. Later he killed his father in an automobile accident. He is sent to an asylum. We gather that these incidents are from his own life. But instead of the asylum, he has ended up at New Carthage College. (Note the symbolic name, Carthage, a city that was destroyed. In times of crisis, Carthage sacrificed some of its own children to Moloch. Perhaps this relates to George's killing of the mythical son.) Naturally George would be interested in the past because of the deaths of his parents having such an effect upon his present life. Therefore, his choice of profession is appropriate.

The college does have overtones of an asylum. The campus is

orderly, and bells chime the hour. The president is somewhat like
the head of such an institution. He is described by George as "a
mouse with red eyes," perhaps the fantasy of an insane man as he
views his keeper.

Underneath their academic appearances, the two teachers have
desperate problems. George looks the part of the stereotyped college professor with a tweed sports coat, baggy pants, a vest-like
sweater, and glasses. But his language is ranting and obscene; he
drinks far too much. Nick also looks the clean-cut young professor,
but is, in actuality, ruthless and concerned more with ambition than
scholarly work.

The sets represent the interior of the characters. George's house
is decaying. It is old, rundown, and very messy. Clothes are strewn
about and there is endless bric-a-brac on the walls. All this clutter is
an appropriate symbol for repressed sexuality. So in the college
(asylum), which is the symbol of intellectual order, we find chaos at
the top level—in the teachers and administration. The college is a
backdrop against which to investigate the lives of these characters.

George is also burdened with tremendous guilt over having accidentally killed his parents. This may be the reason he entered into
the relationship with Martha, who says he married her for all the
symbolic whipping and punishment. Could these deaths, however,
be only as real as the imaginary boy? Another eleaborate game? If
so, it is still interesting that George picked *that* game. By being
humiliated and punished by Martha, George may feel better about
his guilty feelings. He is the "bad boy" who is being punished for his
"crimes."

Note that the "cure" takes place when George kills the fantasy son
(now he has killed his mother, father, and son). He is also killing the
son in him and can perhaps now be a complete man. Note that
George has the symbolic son killed under the same circumstances
(in an automobile accident) in which the father in his novel is killed.

Martha, too, has a hangup about fathers. She wants George to be
like her father, which he can never be. She constantly attacks him
for this. At times, she plays the little girl and we see tender, almost
immature feelings in her. For example, she is upset when George
doesn't want to kiss her after she has been attacking him verbally, so
she pouts like a little girl. Perhaps she too wants to be punished for
her incestuous feelings about "Daddy."

Like George, Martha is a manipulator. In a very revealing

speech, she says, "George, who is good to me, who can keep learning the games we play as quickly as I can change them; who can
make me happy, and I do not wish to be happy. Yes, I do wish to be
happy. George and Martha, sad, sad, sad. Whom I will not forgive
for having come to rest; for having seen me and having said: yes, this
will do; who has made the hideous, the hurting, the insulting mistake of loving me. I must be punished for it. George and Martha,
sad, sad, sad. Some day, some night, some stupid, liquor ridden
night, I will go too far. I'll either break the man's back or I'll push
him off for good, which is what I deserve." Note here that Martha
not only has love/hate feelings but also points out in this speech that
she is in fact a manipulator. She says, in effect, I either shall do this
or I shall do that.

Nichols says of the character of Martha, "The brilliant, overedu-
cated, ball-cutting woman who also has womanly feelings and alternates between them is a very specific type."[3] Women with some of
Martha's characteristics (especially some of her manipulative qualities) can be found in other Nichols films (Mrs. Robinson in *The
Graduate*, Susan in *Carnal Knowledge*, and others).

Nick, the new member of the faculty, is also a manipulator. In a
confession to George, he outlines his strategy for getting ahead. He
will take over a few courses from the older teachers and, perhaps
jokingly, he indicates he will have sex with the wives of a few of the
influential men on the campus (so they can influence their husbands
in his favor) and become an historical "inevitability" for the presi-
dency. When George pushes him a bit too far, he tells George that
he will get him. He married Honey not only because she was supposed to be pregnant, but also because her father had money "to
compensate."

In brilliant parallel construction, Nick is burdened with Honey's
father as George is burdened with Martha's father. Honey's father, a
man of God (where Martha's father is just God-like), became famous
and made money, the compensation (pun intended) for Nick's putting up with her. Martha's father's second wife also had money.

Honey is also a manipulator. She had an hysterical pregnancy,
which she used to manipulate Nick into marrying her. She is constantly pushing her husband's virtues at others. She is frightened of
having children and has no doubt punished Nick sexually by throwing up when he approached her. Nick says that there wasn't any
particular passion between him and Honey, even at the beginning of

their relationship. Honey won't let Nick become a father, perhaps because she may see her own father in a negative way. He was a manipulator, too. As a man of God, he became rich and "spent God's money and saved his own."

Martha's father, like Honey's, is never seen, but he is also presented as a manipulator. Besides refusing to allow George to publish his book, he forced George into a boxing match at a party, and if the president says, "Be nice," one had better comply.

So George and Martha and Nick and Honey all share some of the same characteristics. Both marriages are wracked by self-deception, manipulation, and mutual exploitation. These traits are found in characters in other Nichols' films. But the characters in *Who's Afraid of Virginia Woolf?* are able to come to an understanding about their behavior and some of the motivations behind it.

Each of these characters goes through a purging of the soul very much like a confession to a priest. While Martha reveals her innermost feelings about the child, George is reciting the Requiem. George reveals his childhood to Nick. Nick exposes the reasons for his marriage and reveals his strategy. Honey confesses that she does not really want to have children and is afraid of being alone.

The characters move from mental (and physical) sterility to another psychological state. While George is insisting that the son is dead, Nick says, "Jesus Christ, I understand this." Honey has said truthful things to Nick and herself. And George and Martha may yet change. Nichols suggests this new awareness visually. The whole film has taken place at night, with illumination by artificial light. At the film's conclusion, the real sun begins to shine.

In looking at Nichols' translation of *Who's Afraid of Virginia Woolf?* from a play to a film, one must keep in mind that it would be invalid to judge both by the same standards, since the media are very different. Both have distinctive symbol systems. They may share some of the same symbolic elements (costumes, actors, scenery, music, etc.) but are unique unto themselves and have their own strengths and limitations. The play *Who's Afraid of Virginia Woolf?* is raw material for the film *Who's Afraid of Virginia Woolf?* Each one must be judged on its own merits.

Of course, with such a famous play, Nichols wanted to be true to Albee's intent. He said, "How lucky to get a chance to do the movie, especially since I felt I understood it quite well. How lucky to get a chance to protect it, to some extent. To protect it from being turned into God knows what—'the child was real, but had committed suicide' or whatever else might have been done with it."[4] Nichols did not want to change the intent although he *had* to change symbol systems. If he did not change the symbol systems, he would have had only a mere record of the play, not a *film*, with those symbolic elements unique to film, such as camera movement, editing, black-and-white cinematography. For instance, the play takes place in one room. Nichols moves some of the action to the lawn, a car, and a roadhouse to take advantage of the filmic qualities of these locations. Nichols translated the play into a film and created a very effective work of art. All the elements of the filmic symbol system relate to the "spine" of the work. None is there by chance.

Several concrete items may have been used symbolically to give depth of meaning to the viewer. At the beginning of the film, the dark clouds and full moon predict the storm to come. As George and Martha walk through the campus, a glass greenhouse is seen. The greenhouse may have been shown for three reasons. First, George brings Martha snapdragons (more symbolism, "snap goes the dragon") later in the film, and the viewer is prepared for this gift. The viewer has seen her "Daddy's greenhouse" when George mentions it. Second, the greenhouse is part of the campus milieu at night and adds to the mood. Third, there is a little world of flowers in the greenhouse, all under glass. Like them, the characters in the film also live isolated in their own private world and the glass house indicates that soon their lives will be exposed. One will see through the walls of the characters as one can see through the walls of the greenhouse.

Early in the film Martha chews on a chicken leg, as she symbolically chews on George. Later in the film George, recalling his childhood, sits on a swing in the backyard. We see the grown man sitting on the swing as a young boy would, a visual complement to the words about his childhood. When the characters go to a roadhouse, flashing lights and signs blink in the dark. George and Martha have a tremendous fight, and the lights can be seen blinking behind their heads. When Martha drives the car home and parks it at a crazy angle, one of the turn signals blinks on and off like the lights. Nichols says of this symbol, "And what George sees when he has walked home is that Martha has drunkenly left the car half up on the sidewalk and the directional signal is going, because Martha is a slob, and also because there's a kind of call for help which is Martha, all the time: 'Stop me before I screw more.' "[5]

The darkness itself is a symbol. Outside on the lawn, and outside the roadhouse, the characters are by themselves. They may yell, laugh, scream, drive the car crazily, but no one comes by or sees them. They are alone in the night. Even inside the roadhouse, the proprietor and the hostess are old and detached; they leave the visitors alone. Dawn, of course, means not just that the sun is coming up, but that there is new hope for these characters. Nichols uses other symbolic elements: the somber tones of the characters' appropriate clothing; the sexy outfit Martha changes into for Nick (with pants, of course, since Martha thinks of herself as symbolically wearing the pants in the house); the haunting musical score; the composition of the characters in the living room when Martha is attempting to seduce Nick (Martha seated between Nick and George, thus symbolically coming between them); the parallel between George driving Martha and the guests in a car and George driving his father in a car before the accident; and finally the inclusion of a fireplace which is not lit in the frame behind Martha as she learns about her son's death. Martha's (the dragon's) fire is also out.

Several motifs run through the film, unify it, and may function symbolically. The first is the phrase *Who's Afraid of Virginia Woolf?* itself. Not only is this the title, but it is used throughout the film in relation to a gag at the faculty party the characters had attended. It is also used at the end of the film, when George asks Martha, "Who's afraid of Virginia Woolf?" and she answers, "I am, George." Actually, the phrase is an allusion to the song from Walt Disney's *The Three Little Pigs*, in which the pigs sang, "Who's afraid of the big bad wolf?" I don't think that this means that the characters are slobs (pigs) who are trying to keep Martha's Daddy (the wolf) away from the door. However, changing the "big bad wolf" to Virginia Woolf certainly relates to the intellectual college milieu. Also, after recurring attacks of insanity, Virginia Woolf committed suicide. George and Martha may well be afraid of their death-in-life. The best explanation is mentioned by Malcolm Boyd in *The Christian Century*. He sees the meaning as "who's afraid to go on without any of the old props?"[6] The props, of course, are the mythical son, and the games that George and Martha play, manipulations, and anything that prevents one from seeing clearly and relating honestly.

The second motif is very subtle. That is the doorbell chimes, which are used as motivating factors throughout the film. At the beginning of the film, as the credits are superimposed over George and Martha walking home, music is heard. An instrument sounds like chimes, which introduces the motif and foreshadows the action. The chimes are next heard as the doorbell when Nick and Honey come to visit. They are heard again when George goes outside to the swing. The door hits against the chimes as he opens it. Much later, when George breaks into the house after Martha has locked him out, the door again hits the chimes. This causes Honey, who has been sleeping in the car, to ask him what the bells were. This gives George the idea to tell Martha that a telegram was delivered which said that their son had been killed. George also starts the last phase of the film when he rings the doorbell and then presents Martha with snapdragons. The chimes were a motif in Albee's play, of course, but in the film they are introduced in the musical score. This is what Nichols meant by ". . . the stronger the spine, the stronger the backbone of the thing that you're making, the more—whether openly or secretly—everything that happens is tied into that backbone. The more solid it is, maybe the truer it is."[7] The chimes on the music track are secretly tied into the spine and make the work of art more solid.

A third symbolic motif is the drinking which is going on constantly throughout the film. George and Martha and Nick and Honey are symbolically drowning, not just in liquor, but in the way that they relate to each other. In order to save himself and Martha from this symbolic drowning, George symbolically kills the fantasy child that binds him and Martha together. Now they will have to swim in reality, not drown in fantasy. And there is some question whether they can do this. The notion of a man drowning is central to the film and the play. It is heard twice in the lines. When Martha refers to George as a portrait of a man drunk, he says, "I am not drowning." In referring to George and his relationship with their son, Martha says, "a drowning man takes down those nearest, and he tried."

This is not the only Nichols' film in which the image of a person drowning symbolically and trying to save himself is seen. This image is found in all Nichols' films to one extent or another and seems to be one of his obsessive motifs. In *The Graduate* Benjamin is drowning among objects. We also see him at the bottom of a swimming pool in a diving suit "fading away." In *Catch-22* Yossarian is afraid of drowning in the ocean if his plane crashes. He is also afraid of drowning in inhumanity and chaos. In *Carnal Knowledge* Jonathan cannot save himself from symbolic, moral drowning. The water is frozen, and his ideal woman skates on ice. Jonathan finally has only sexual, not loving, feelings toward women. In *The Day of the Dolphin* Dr. Jake Terrell cannot swim to safety with his perfect creatures, the dolphins. In *The Fortune* Freddie is symbolically drowning in her relationship with two men. This is shown in concrete terms when they place her in a chest and drop her into the sea. She escapes the watery death, but cannot escape the symbolic death-in-life. In "Family," a television series which is a Mike Nichols Production, it was established that the thirteen-year-old daughter Buddy was once saved from drowning in a river by her father and older brother Willie. They could not save her younger brother Timmy. In one episode, she is afraid she will drown if she dives off a diving board into a pool. She dives into the water when she thinks no one is around. She swims for herself, but is given a helping hand by Willie.

The importance of the "drowning" motif shows one of the ways that the film concentrates on George. It is George whom Martha pushes too far, breaking their rules by her sexual liaison with Nick. And it is George who finally kills the child and frees them both. In order to concentrate on George, Nichols uses a particularly cinematic device, the "subjective camera." Frequently the camera becomes, as it were, the eyes of George, and the viewer sees only what George sees and sees it from George's point of view. It is George, for example, who sees the car with the flashing light at a crazy angle in the driveway. Occasionally Nichols employs the device with other characters, but primarily with George. This is a way that filmmakers have of getting the viewer inside a character's head and having the viewer identify with a character. Nichols' camera becomes subjective when George approaches Martha with the toy shotgun. It moves toward the back of Martha's head from George's viewpoint. Another time, he and the camera look up at the bedroom window, where the shadows of Martha and Nick can be seen making love. The subjective camera is also used when Honey is being swung in a circle by George.

Nichols has said that every element must relate to the "spine" of the film. This of course includes camera angle, distance, and movement. What sets Nichols apart from lesser filmmakers is that his use of the camera is motivated. He does not move the camera arbitrarily. For example, the camera follows George when he moves across the room. The movement is motivated. As George describes his boyhood days, the camera moves toward him, for the viewer wants to hear more and is becoming involved. The viewer is seldom aware of the different camera distances, angles, and movements (and the camera moves very often), for, being motivated, they become part of the story Nichols is telling and do not call attention to themselves. They are an integrated part of the filmic symbol system that Nichols uses so well.

For example, camera distance is used to show that George is very lonely. When George goes outside and sits on the swing, Nick is watching him from the back door of the house. The camera shares Nick's point of view: in extreme long shot, it shows the entire dark backyard, with George, sitting on the swing, very far away in a patch of light. There is a bit of mist floating by, perhaps made by the smoke of George's cigarette. In this way, the camera distance denotes where George is and also connotes how lonely he is.

Camera angle is used symbolically when Martha is in the roadhouse telling how her father would not let George publish his autobiographical novel. She is hitting drums and the bandstand with a drumstick just as she is symbolically hitting George with her words; the gesture is an indication of Nichols' genius. The camera is down low looking up at Martha; from this angle she looks very powerful. The opposite angle is used when Martha cries over the death of her son. The camera is placed high and looks down at her; she is made to look small and weak.

An example of excellent camera movement with no cutting is found at the end of the film. George asks Martha "Who's afraid of Virginia Woolf?" and she answers, "I am, George, I am." The camera is on a close-up of George. It follows him as he walks away from it toward Martha, and as he stands by Martha, it remains on a medium shot of the two of them. It slowly moves toward them when Martha places her hand on George's hand. The camera then moves past them to show the trees outside the window in the morning light. Here, in one continuous running, the camera has moved in as they say significant words, has moved onto their hands to present this loving detail to the viewer, and then finally has moved to the dawn outside and its hope for the future.

As with the use of the camera, Nichols' cutting is also motivated. Often, it is motivated by lines: one character says something, and then there is a cut to the next character talking. Often it is motivated by looks: a character looks somewhere, and there is a cut to what he sees. Often it is motivated by action: there is a cut to a character reacting to a line or to a movement. But it must be remembered that all these elements of the filmic symbol system are not isolated and do not happen one at a time. They all must work together in each shot and in the entire film. The camera in long shot is important in making George look lonely on the swing, but it functions along with the melancholy music, the lighting of the mist, the dark backyard, and Burton's position on the swing itself. The shots that precede it (Nick coming on the porch) and the shots that follow it (Nick coming toward George) all add to the total effect of the film.

Even the locations where the picture was filmed were chosen with the total effect of the film in mind. Nichols chose to shoot on location in Northampton, Massachusetts. He thought that it would help the actors and the tone of the work if he used a real college campus. The atmosphere of the picture is helped tremendously. Nichols wisely chose black-and-white film instead of color film which tends to look "pretty." With the story of *Who's Afraid of Virginia Woolf?* prettiness would detract from the "spine" of the film. Black and white helped to lessen the attractiveness of Richard Burton and Elizabeth Taylor. It also helped symbolically to isolate the universe created in the film from the colorful real world. The wide contrast ratio of black-and-white film, with its many shades of gray, also reinforced the emotional tones and depths of the characters.[8]

Lighting was carefully done. The lighting was harsh in the battle scenes and soft in tender moments. When George goes to the closet to get a toy gun, he knocks the naked light bulb and it swings back and forth, making him look demonic, a device similar to the one used in Alfred Hitchcock's *Psycho*, when the light swings over the skull of Mrs. Bates in the cellar. In a softer moment, when dawn approaches, George turns off the lights in the room (the artificial lights equating with the artificial qualities of his and Martha's relationship) and real light from the sun enters the room. Lighting and cinematography helped produce beautiful atmospheric shots. For example, as George and Martha enter the house, bugs fly around the overhead light on the porch. The smoke from George's cigarette encircles him as he sits on the swing in a pool of light. Lights at the roadhouse flash in the dark, producing a sense of loneliness.

Nichols has always been a fine director of actors, and I feel that the quality of acting in this film is high. Acting is an element of the symbol system and must be seen in the context of the total work of art. Richard Burton and Elizabeth Taylor are very well known and yet to Nichols' credit these superstars rarely overwhelm the other elements of the symbol system. Burton as George and Taylor as Martha were believable in the film as were Segal as Nick and Dennis as Honey. (Elizabeth Taylor and Sandy Dennis won Academy Awards for their performances.) In my opinion, all gave excellent performances.

Nichols seemed to have been constantly aware of the film's "spine," and the elements of the symbol system were used to relate to the film's inner meaning. The elements are so tightly knit together and work so well that one can view *Who's Afraid of Virginia Woolf?* again and again and learn more each time about the complexity and rightness of the work. This artistic control and feeling of rightness can be found in all Nichols' films.

As we have seen, *Who's Afraid of Virginia Woolf?* ends on a note of hope; Martha admits that she is afraid to go on without the old props. She holds George's hand, and the sun rises. However, even with illusions stripped away and new understanding on the part of all the characters, it will still be, as George says, "Sunday tomorrow, all day." Even with rays of sunlight and hope, one is left with the feeling that on this Sunday, and on Sundays to follow, George and Martha will not change enough. She will still be the president's daughter; he will still not publish his novel or take over the History Department. The characters may indeed relapse into different games. There may not be enough changed. It is not a completely optimistic, happy ending.

If these characters, however, remain trapped at New Carthage, at least members of the audience may leave, perhaps moved by Nichols' vision.

The characters are larger than life. Their problems and illusions are simplified, organized, dramatized, and amplified for us. By understanding these characters, we may be able to understand ourselves and others better. Nichols' statement on one part of the human condition is universal enough to provide the viewer with insight, and this is one of the functions of art.

Who's Afraid of Virginia Woolf? had an impact on our culture and on film history apart from its intrinsic merits. The film was a breakthrough for artistic freedom and a defeat for censorship. When Ernest Lehman first wrote the script, he tried to retain the flavor of Albee's play, but recognizing the historic climate of film censorship, had also tried to launder it. After Nichols and Lehman had worked more than six months on the script, they decided they were being dishonest. "Disguising profanity with clean but suggestive phrases is really dirtier," said Nichols. " . . . We feel the language in *Woolf?* is essential to the fabric, it reveals who the people are and how they lived."[9] Nichols and Lehman discarded most of the revisions and went back to using much of Albee's dialogue. They felt that the artistic intent of the film would overcome any objections.

As a hedge against censorship, Nichols could have shot alternate covering shots which substituted softened language in the more controversial scenes. But Nichols refused this safeguard and this was one way that he protected the artistic integrity of his work.[10] On May 25, 1966, Jack L. Warner, president of Warner Brothers, announced that the film would be released for adults only. All contracts with theaters exhibiting the film would include a clause prohibiting anyone under the age of eighteen from seeing the film unless accompanied by an adult. The clause was the first ever adopted by Warner Brothers. According to the *New York Times* (May 26, 1966), Mr. Warner said that the film was made because it had something to say to adults. He added, "We do not think this a film for children"(p. 57).

The Motion Picture Association of America's Production Code Administration, the Association's West Coast Censorship body, refused to give its seal of approval to the film unless some of its dialogue was removed. Jack L. Warner refused. Geoffrey Shurlock, the code's administrator, withheld the seal pending its review by the Motion Picture Association of America's Product Code Review Board. On June 10, the board voted to approve the film and give it a seal. The board, which exempted *Who's Afraid of Virginia Woolf?* from code standards on dialogue, was made up of Jack J. Valenti, who had just become president of the Motion Picture Association of America, five representatives of producing-distributing companies that are association members, four exhibitors, and one independent producer. Reasons for exempting the film were that "it is not designed to be prurient," and that "it is largely a reproduction of the play that won the New York Drama Critics Award of 1963 and played throughout the country." The board emphasized that the exemption "means exactly that—approval of material in a specific, important film that would not be approved for a film of lesser quality, or a film determined to exploit language for language's sake.

This exemption does not mean that the floodgates are open for language or other material." There was no indication how each member of the eleven-man review board voted. According to its governing procedure, however, exemptions can be granted only when voted by a two-thirds majority. Mr. Valenti, who had earlier upheld the code administrator and thus opened the way for Warner Brothers to appeal to the review board, had but one vote as a review board member.[11]

The film was also shown to representatives of the National Catholic Office for Motion Pictures, formerly the Legion of Decency. Eighty-one volunteer college-educated raters from the Church attended a screening and wrote reports for the head of the office, Monsignor Thomas F. Little, and his chief associate, Father Patrick J. Sullivan. Father Little and Father Sullivan both saw the film twice. Of the eighty-one reports, the overwhelming majority were in favor of approving the film. Monsignor Little announced that the film would get an A-4 rating, "morally unobjectionable for adults, with reservations."

"We put Who's Afraid of Virginia Woolf? in what we call our 'think film' category," the Monsignor explained. Other films in that category at the time included Darling, 8½, and La Dolce Vita. The Monsignor also said, "It is all right to use erotic elements when everything jells in artistic integrity. Dean Martin doing the same things in The Silencers most certainly would not be approved."[12]

There is no doubt that Who's Afraid of Virginia Woolf? helped film move toward what Bosley Crowther calls a "relatively free and adult screen."[13] In fact, The Pawnbroker (1965) seems to be the only film from this period to have had as much influence on censorship standards. It was at first refused a seal because it contained two short scenes of nudity. Later, the Code Review Board overruled the code administrator and granted an exemption from code requirements. Thus, The Pawnbroker did for images what Who's Afraid of Virginia Woolf? did for dialogue. These two pictures not only affected what was going to be on the screen in the future but also eventually led to new standards within the industry and to the film classification system itself. Alfie (1966), in which an abortion figured prominently, also was given an exemption (and thus approval) shortly after Who's Afraid of Virginia Woolf? was approved.

Audiences all over the United States were, as Vincent Canby put it, "not afraid of big bad Woolf." He wrote in the New York Times

(June 25, 1966, p. 21) that two thousand watched the film and emerged unshocked. Whatever the moods and values of the public at a certain point in history, the fact remains that *Who's Afraid of Virginia Woolf?* possesses qualities that separate a large artistic accomplishment from a small. It remains and will remain a work of art despite changing public morality. Writing on *Who's Afraid of Virginia Woolf?* in *America*, Moira Walsh makes good sense: "The moral impact of an art form depends, not on its subject matter but on how soundly and coherently the artist's vision transcends the subject matter."[14]

Finally, two critical theories about *Who's Afraid of Virginia Woolf?* need to be reviewed.

A review for *Newsweek* advanced the idea that:

Albee is using his harrowing heterosexual couples as surrogates for homosexual partners having a vicious, narcissistic, delightedly self-indulgent spat. He has not really written about men and women, with a potential for love and sex, however withered the potential may be. He has written about sabertoothed humans who cannot reproduce and who need to draw buckets of blood before they can feel compassion for each other.[15]

Nichols disposes of this theory well:

If Edward Albee wanted to write a play about four men, he would and he could. He wrote a play about two men, *The Zoo Story*. Also, when you're attacking the problem of the play, it becomes an insane idea. What do these people propose? That the son of the president of the university has lived for twenty-one years with his boyfriend and he is entertaining for the evening the new science teacher with his boyfriend? It has no meaning. The whole thing disintegrates.

So much of the play is about Martha's disappointment in George's not living up to her father and not taking over the university. Do they assume that Albee tacked all this on because he was deprived of his original idea? Then at the end you would discover that the entire play was tacked on, because with the exception of that truthful thing about the child—that it's impossible for two men to have a child—there is nothing in the text to substantiate it.[16]

Nichols goes on to say that there are things in *Who's Afraid of Virginia Woolf?* that must be true in homosexual relationships, but that also must be true in heterosexual relationships.

The second interpretation is that the film is an allegory about the character and illusion of the American dream of a new ideal society as the dream emerged at the time of the Revolution.[17] (Albee earlier did also write a short, satirical play called *The American Dream.*) George and Martha stand for George and Martha Washington. George killed his mother (England) and his child is the "American Dream" never realized. The real Virginia Woolf was a novelist who was also a social critic of English culture. The allegorical meaning continues in its complexity.

This is a useful frame of reference for analysis, but there are problems with it. George kills his mother, yes, but accidentally. In American history the Revolution was neither accidental nor did it destroy England. And I doubt if Albee or Nichols really thought of Martha as "the vulgar mercantile class of pre-revolutionary America" nor George as "America's intellectual heritage."[18] Such a frame of reference is useful, however, in exploring the many overtones created by *Who's Afraid of Virginia Woolf?* However, I feel this allegory falls into the realm of departure criticism, where a critic takes a work and then departs to his own set of ideas and values, interpreting the work to fit them. It is amusing to have our first President and his wife's name used in this decadent situation, but it is unconvincing to read into it any more than the obvious point that America (a new Carthage) is going downhill.

Who's Afraid of Virginia Woolf? cost about six million dollars to produce. What is important is not the cost, but the fact that Nichols was given complete creative freedom on the film. It is indeed a Nichols' film. Nichols collaborated on the film with many creative and talented people; he had excellent raw material in Albee's play. But it was his personal vision that guided and controlled the film, and he was ultimately responsible for the images on the screen. Without Mike Nichols, it would have been a very different film.

3

The Graduate

IN 1967 NICHOLS DIRECTED his second film, *The Graduate*. He also directed Lillian Hellman's *The Little Foxes* for the Repertory Theatre at Lincoln Center. He followed that with Neil Simon's play, *Plaza Suite*, for which he won his fourth Tony award for best director.

The Graduate won Mike Nichols an Academy Award for best film director and was very popular.

The story concerns Benjamin (Dustin Hoffman), a whiz at college in both studies and athletics. He is not only captain of the debate team but also a track star. After graduation, he returns to California from his Eastern college and appears zombie-like to his parents, their friends, and the values they live by. He is seduced by Mrs. Robinson (Anne Bancroft), the wife of his father's business partner, but he seems to have started this relationship out of boredom more than anything else. Mrs. Robinson's daughter Elaine (Katharine Ross) is currently attending college. One kiss from Elaine changes Benjamin from passivity to action. He now pursues Elaine and, overcoming all odds, rescues her at a church just after she marries a medical student. Benjamin and Elaine (she still in her wedding gown), leave together on a bus.

Nichols says of the story:

I think it was the story of a not particularly bright, not particularly remarkable, but worthy kid drowning among objects and things, committing moral suicide by allowing himself to be used finally like an object or a thing by Mrs. Robinson, because he doesn't have the moral or intellectual resources to do what a large percentage of other kids like him do—to rebel, to march, to demonstrate, to turn on. Just drowning.

Then finding himself to some extent, finding part of himself that he hadn't found, through connection with a girl. Finding passion because of impossi-

45

Dustin Hoffman (Benjamin) and Anne Bancroft (Mrs. Robinson) in The Graduate.

Courtesy of the Museum of Modern Art/Film Stills Archive

bility. Impossibility always leads to passion and vice versa. Going from passion to a kind of insanity. Saving himself temporarily from being an object, through the passion and insanity. Getting what he thinks he wanted and beginning to subside back into the same world in which he has to live, with not enough changed. I think that's the story.[1]

In order to understand how Nichols articulates this story in filmic terms, I will analyze in detail each of the major scenes, concentrating on three elements: color, music, and visual motif, although other symbolic elements will also be mentioned when appropriate to the analysis.

Color may be used by Nichols to comment on the characters' personalities, the quality of their environment, and relationships between the characters and their environment. Colors may reinforce, hint at, and suggest truths that plot and dialogue establish.

Music is used symbolically in several ways. It may be part of the action on the screen and come from a logical source. For example, Mrs. Robinson switches on the stereo and plays a sexy Latin song, which relates to her seduction of Benjamin. Or, it may be used as background music with no logical source. For example, a guitar provides rhythmic accompaniment to Benjamin's desperate search for Elaine. Finally, it may be used as a "Greek chorus," during which Simon and Garfunkle's songs, "The Sound of Silence," "Mrs. Robinson," "Scarborough Fair/Canticle," "April Come She Will," and others (some written before the film was made), comment symbolically on the action. For example, during the first scenes of the film when Benjamin arrives in the Los Angeles airport, the song "The Sound of Silence" is sung, with words that describe Benjamin's feelings and the environment into which Benjamin is heading:

> (1st verse)
> Hello darkness my old friend,
> I've come to talk with you again,
> Because a vision softly creeping,
> left its seeds while I was sleeping,
> And the vision that was planted,
> in my brain still remains
> within the sound of silence.
> (3rd verse)
> And in the naked light I saw
> ten thousand people, maybe more.

People talking without speaking,
people hearing without listening
People writing songs that voices never share
and no one dare
Disturb the sound of silence.
("Sound of Silence" © 1964 Paul Simon. Used by Permission)

Visual motifs are objects that reappear throughout a film and give it unity. They have symbolic significance. For example, water is a visual motif in *The Graduate*, which relates to Nichols' statement about Benjamin "just drowning." The clearest use of this is Benjamin in a diving suit standing at the bottom of a pool. As the camera moves away from him, he gets smaller and smaller as the water obscures him. Several such motifs that unify the film and enhance the meaning will be analyzed.

Many colors, costumes, and objects that Nichols uses in *The Graduate* are representative of an upper-middle class Southern California milieu. These colors, costumes and objects may have more than a literal meaning. They may have a deeper, symbolic meaning.

The film opens on a close-shot of Benjamin's face. This immediately shows the audience that Benjamin is alone. There is a zoom out to reveal that Benjamin is seated in an airplane. The seats and the overhead rack are white. White will be used later in the film many times. It connotes a sterile, cold environment. Through the plane's loudspeaker, the pilot tells the passengers that they are about to begin their descent into Los Angeles. This establishes the place where the film will begin, and the word "descent" has a denotative and a connotative meaning. It denotes the landing. It connotes a going down, perhaps even into hell.

Benjamin moves alone in the crowd and "The Sound of Silence" is sung. The credits are superimposed against white walls. Benjamin has a black suitcase and is carrying a white coat. He is wearing a gray suit, black-and-white tie, and white shirt. The color motif continues in Benjamin's house, where Benjamin is seen staring into his aquarium. He tells his father that he is concerned about his future, that he wants it to be different. But his father is interested in getting him downstairs. His parents are throwing a welcome-home/graduation party for him, and he does not wish to come downstairs to attend. His mother is dressed in white. He and his father are dressed in gray, black, and white.

His tie contains golden brown, which may relate to a later scene, where he and Elaine at Berkeley both wear brown coats that visually connect them. He may have a bit of warmth and rebellion in him as suggested by the warm color in his tie. Or the gold may stand for money, a symbol of his parent's values.

There is a picture of a clown on the upstairs wall: and as he and his parents go downstairs, the camera holds on the clown for a bit. The clown symbolically stands for Benjamin. The walls of his home are white. The furniture is white and black. The swimming pool is a shimmering blue. The party guests are dressed primarily in blues, blacks, and whites. So Nichols may be suggesting through color the kind of environment Benjamin is in, a cold, sterile, and unfeeling one. Benjamin himself is photographed in close-up as he moves through the guests. The camera follows him, concentrating on his face. Other faces swim into the frame only when he encounters them. He is really alone, Nichols shows us. It looks as if he is swimming through the guests. The next scene reinforces this idea, as he goes to his room and stares again at fish swimming in his blue aquarium. The fish are swimming alone as he was swimming alone at the party downstairs as conveyed by the camera. The camera movement and the aquarium reinforce Nichols' idea of Benjamin symbolically drowning. A model of a diver at the bottom of the aquarium prefigures the later picture of Benjamin in his diving suit at the bottom of the pool. The images purposely reflect the idea of Benjamin symbolically drowning not in water, but in the values and mores of his subculture, the materialistic generation with their swimming pools, color television, and multiple cars.

Benjamin is given a diving suit and a sports car. In fact, in terms of objects, he is given everything. The rich subculture believes in consumption. It has been described as "the plastic society," and in fact, during the party, one of the "cold fish" takes Benjamin aside to give him the word for future success, which turns out to be "plastics."

So Benjamin is staring at the fish when Mrs. Robinson enters, wearing a shiny, reptile-like black dress and carrying a black fur coat. Nichols wishes to show her animal-like nature and has her constantly dressed in animal skin patterns of one sort or another throughout the film.

She asks Benjamin to drive her home in the new car his parents gave him for his graduation. He gives her the keys and requests that she drive herself home. She finally persuades Benjamin to drive her and tosses the keys in the aquarium so that he must fish them out. This indicates her cruel nature and is a very nice symbolic touch on Nichols' part. The keys have the sign-symbol characteristic. They will start the car, but they will also start Benjamin on his way to understanding. Mrs. Robinson holds the symbolic keys to Benjamin's emergence, and she makes Benjamin "get his feet wet" (his hand, actually), by reaching for the keys in the aquarium.

At the Robinson home, the color symbolism continues. The walls are white, the floor black. Mrs. Robinson turns on sexy Latin music. She confesses to Benjamin that she is an alcoholic (she drowns in liquor), and there is very clever dialogue between the two as Mrs. Robinson carefully attempts her seduction of Benjamin. It is like a Nichols and May sketch, with Mrs. Robinson seducing Benjamin, saying exactly the opposite of what she is doing.

She invites Benjamin upstairs to see the portrait of her daughter, Elaine, in Elaine's room, and he reluctantly goes with her. Elaine's room is done in pink and white. Pink, a feminine color of the warm, red spectrum, but suggestive of youth or immaturity, is Elaine's color motif. In the portrait, she is dressed in pink, and there is a pink background surrounding her. Perhaps there is a connection between her portrait as the upper middle class ideal girl and the picture of the clown in Benjamin's home which may represent him.

Mrs. Robinson asks Benjamin to unzip her dress. At this moment Elaine's portrait appears between Benjamin and Mrs. Robinson. As he unzips her dress, the camera moves and loses the picture of Elaine. Mrs. Robinson's underwear continues the animal-skin motif. Her bra and slip are of black-and-white leopard skin. Mrs. Robinson asks Benjamin to go downstairs and bring up her purse. She asks that he leave it in Elaine's room. What follows is one of those remarkable shots that has strong connotative as well as denotative meaning. Benjamin is looking at Elaine's portrait. The portrait is covered by glass. The camera is on the portrait when, in the reflection in the glass, the bedroom door opens and Mrs. Robinson enters in the nude. As she opens the door, her image blots out Elaine's face.

There are two meanings here. On the denotative, or sign, level, she has entered the room. On the connotative, or symbolic, level, she has blotted out Elaine in Benjamin's mind. The placement of the camera here lets the viewer become aware of this overshadowing. Benjamin's head turns to look at her and this is repeated three times in three quick cuts to indicate his shock. There are now several quick cuts between Benjamin's face and various parts of Mrs. Robinson's nude body. As Benjamin's eyes move, there is a shot of what he sees. Nichols purposely has Mrs. Robinson seen through Benjamin's eyes so the viewer identifies with Benjamin, gets into his mind, so to speak, and sees what he sees. The film unfolds from Benjamin's point of view, and Nichols rarely has a scene in the entire picture without Benjamin in it. We never see Mrs. Robinson and Elaine talking about Benjamin, for instance. Benjamin is with us, from the first shot of the film to the last.

Mrs. Robinson locks the door (she still holds the symbolic keys), and says that she will be available to Benjamin at any time. When Benjamin hears Mr. Robinson's car outside, he unlocks the door and rushes past her. Benjamin goes downstairs, Mr. Robinson enters, and invites Benjamin to have a drink with him. Mr. Robinson wears a tan shirt under a white sweater. The tan may indicate a connection with Benjamin here. Both are manipulated by Mrs. Robinson, and Mr. Robinson may not be a totally "negative" person. As he tells Benjamin to sow some wild oats, Nichols places the camera so that Mrs. Robinson is seen coming into the room between Benjamin and her husband. Symbolically, she does come between their friendship. Benjamin leaves, and does not act on Mrs. Robinson's invitation until he is motivated by the diving-suit scene.

The viewer is invited to "get inside Benjamin's head" once again with this scene, shot primarily through the subjective camera technique where the camera becomes the eyes of the subject. Benjamin has been given a diving suit for his birthday by his parents. The camera is inside the face mask of Benjamin's rubber diving suit, and we see from Benjamin's point of view his father wildly gesturing at him to come outside the house and to get into the pool. We don't hear what his father is saying, only Benjamin's heavy breathing. There are guests around the pool, dressed mostly in white, and the pool itself is blue, continuing the cold, sterile color motifs. Ben's father is dressed in blue. One person does have on a yellow shirt—perhaps a symbol of affluence or cowardice. As Benjamin enters the pool, his father pushes him (the camera) under the water. The subjective camera becomes objective and finds Benjamin standing on the bottom of the pool. The camera pulls back until the viewer almost loses sight of him standing there. He becomes smaller and smaller as the blue water obscures him. Benjamin is shown symbolically drowning, fading away, becoming nothing.

To save himself from this "drowning," Benjamin calls Mrs. Robinson from a phone booth in the next shot, and we hear his voice before the cut to him on the phone, clearly showing the connection between the symbolic drowning and his motivation to call her. Benjamin and the guests at the hotel continue to wear primarily cold colors (blue, white, gray, black). In the hotel, the camera becomes Benjamin's eyes once more as he sees a desk clerk. The clerk asks him, "Are you here for an affair, sir?" By "affair," of course, he meant a party, not a sexual rendezvous.

Mrs. Robinson's association with an animal motif continues as she comes to the hotel dressed in black with a coat of animal skin. She is first seen reflected in the glass top of a table in the bar where Benjamin is sitting (the image here relates to her earlier reflection in Elaine's portrait). The Latin music being played echoes the music at the Robinson home during the attempted seduction.

The hotel has a red carpet. The red probably indicates that there is some sex underlying the events in this scene. Bluish-white is the color of the hotel room. Mrs. Robinson now wears a black-and-white slip in the pattern of a giraffe skin. Nichols has created a cold environment.

This scene continues the theme of the innocent graduating into maturity. As Benjamin expresses guilty feelings about sleeping with her, Mrs. Robinson suggests that he is a virgin (innocent). In order to prove his maturity, Benjamin will consummate the affair. As he slams the door, the screen goes *black*, "The Sound of Silence" is heard, with the words, "Hello darkness, my old friend." During this song and the following "April Come She Will," a series of scenes cut between the hotel room and Benjamin at home to indicate that time is passing as the affair continues. "The Sound of Silence" indicates that there is little besides physical communication between Benjamin and Mrs. Robinson. "April Come She Will" indicates that the affair is becoming stagnant.

The cool colors continue in these scenes. In one of them, Benjamin is in the pool on a black raft and is wearing dark sunglasses. He gets out of the pool, sees his mother in a black-and-white zebra outfit (which connects her to Mrs. Robinson and the sterile subculture) and Benjamin himself puts on a white shirt. The white is used as a connecting link between Benjamin's home and the hotel room where Benjamin is seen in a white shirt and white underpants. Nichols connects Benjamin at home and Benjamin with Mrs. Robinson by clever cutting between the two places as time passes. For example, Benjamin in the pool leaps up on his raft. There is a cut and he lands not on the raft, but on Mrs. Robinson in bed. His father's voice asks, "Benjamin, what are you doing?" Benjamin turns toward the camera and the next shot is of his father at poolside looking down at him. The scene is back at the pool and the camera has again become Benjamin's eyes.

Occasionally other colors are seen. There is a bit of yellow seen on Mr. Robinson which perhaps suggests cowardice or affluence. When Benjamin's mother insists that she doesn't want to pry into his affairs, but asks him why he spends so much time away from home, he cuts his finger and we see a bit of red. Perhaps he thinks of the sexual encounters with Mrs. Robinson here. Thus the red, a passionate color, may be connected with sexual anxiety. But the predominant colors are cool indeed.

In a brutal scene where Benjamin tries to talk to Mrs. Robinson, she makes him promise not to take Elaine out. She indicates that he is not good enough for her daughter. (During part of this scene, incidentally, Benjamin is wearing a brown coat—which will be echoed by the brown coat Elaine wears in a later scene.) Benjamin calls her a broken-down alcoholic whom he sees out of boredom. They both apologize to each other. Benjamin shows a definite lack of sensitivity here (Mrs. Robinson may be jealous of her youthful daughter), but so does Mrs. Robinson (Benjamin may wish more than just sexual satisfaction). Note the formality. He always calls her Mrs. Robinson, and never uses her first name. She calls him Benjamin, not the less formal "Ben."

Benjamin agrees not to take Elaine out. His parents threaten to have all the Robinsons over for dinner unless he sees Elaine. He asks her out, apparently to avoid the party. But one must remember the words of "April Come She Will":

> April, come she will
> When streams are ripe and swelled with rain;
> May, she will stay,
> Resting in my arms again.
> June, she'll change her tune,

In restless walks she'll prowl the night;
July, she will fly,
And give no warning to her flight.
August, die she must,
The autumn winds blow chilly and cold;
September I'll remember.
A love once new has now grown old. ("April Come She Will"
© 1965 Paul Simon. Used by Permission.)

This song describes the course of Benjamin's affair with Mrs. Robinson. The song is true to the time period—the affair lasts over the summer and ends in September, with Elaine going back to school. It starts sexually, but gives way to boredom. Benjamin tries to talk with Mrs. Robinson, but it seems that what she wants is sex. During this affair, there is much walking about in the hotel room, hence she "prowls the night." Finally, the last line . . . "a love once new has now grown old" sums up what has happened between Benjamin and Mrs. Robinson and may provide a subconscious motivation for his calling on Elaine.

When Benjamin comes to pick up Elaine, the colors are mainly in the cold range. Mrs. Robinson is in black. Mr. Robinson wears a pinkish shirt, which may relate him to Elaine here, as he may be concerned about Elaine. Benjamin wears a white-and-black striped coat, blue shirt, and black tie. Elaine wears a pink dress and carries a white coat. This pink, Elaine's color, recalls her white and pink room and her pink portrait.

As Benjamin enters the living room to pick up Elaine, Mrs. Robinson is sitting on the sofa watching "The Newlywed Game" on television. The girl on the show also wears pink, and the boy and the girl on the show connect Benjamin and Elaine in Mrs. Robinson's and the viewer's mind and foreshadow the ending. The parallel that leaps to mind intensifies Mrs. Robinson's anger and is indicative of Nichols' mastery of filmic symbolism. The question on "The Newlywed Game," asked, appropriately enough over a close-up of Mrs. Robinson's face, is "What is your wife's most unusual habit?"

As Benjamin and Elaine leave, a close-up of Mrs. Robinson's face slowly dissolves into the back of Elaine's head in Benjamin's car. Elaine is now replacing her with Benjamin.

Benjamin takes Elaine to a strip joint deliberately to humiliate her. His motivation may be to preserve his relationship with Mrs. Robinson, but it also allows him to hurt her as he was hurt by his father (in the diving suit incident) and by others in the subculture.

There is a reddish curtain in the strip joint (red again suggesting sex). The stripper wears white (and little of it). When Benjamin compares Elaine to the stripper, Elaine cries. When Benjamin takes off his sunglasses, he symbolically "sees" clearly for the first time. Red continues to be the dominant color as Elaine leaves suddenly and runs down the street. Benjamin finally catches her near a poster with red and pink in it.

He tells the crying Elaine that he is not really what he seems to be, and they kiss, a very loving, tender kiss, compared with his behavior in his relationship with Mrs. Robinson.

Benjamin and Elaine go to a drive-in restaurant. He talks seriously to her about his feelings, telling her that he is not the way he seems. She listens and understands. Simon and Garfunkle sing the words "Does your boss just mention that you ought to shop around?" indicating that Benjamin and Elaine are shopping around not only for new relationships but also for new values. ("The Big Bright Green Pleasure Machine" © 1966 Paul Simon. Used by Permission.) Benjamin raises the top of his convertible to shut out the noise of the drive-in so that he and Elaine can talk better. The viewer does not hear what they say and words are not necessary. The relationship is developed visually. Isolated in the car they are separated from the subculture.

Benjamin and Elaine drive to her home, and he obviously doesn't want to go in. He suggests they go somewhere for a drink, and Elaine suggests the Taft Hotel, the same place where Benjamin and Mrs. Robinson have been meeting. As the car pulls away, the camera tilts up to the windows on the second floor of the house, perhaps where Mrs. Robinson has been watching. At the hotel, Nichols shows a porter in a red vest (sex is ever present there). There is an hilarious exchange between Benjamin and the members of the hotel staff, who know him as Mr. Gladstone (a pseudonym he used when visiting the hotel with Mrs. Robinson) and between Benjamin and Miss DeWitte, who thinks he is Mr. Braniff (a name he used when he accidentally became involved in a party at the hotel).

Benjamin and Elaine sit in his car outside the hotel. He tells her that she is the first person he has liked in a long time. She asks if he is having an affair with someone, and he answers yes, but that it is all over now (he decides here to end it). During this scene, headlights from other cars bounce off of Benjamin's red car and create flashes of pink, almost an aura of pinks, around the couple. He is totally caught up in Elaine's spell, and this is shown visually with the use of Elaine's color.

They go to Elaine's house, but do not kiss each other goodnight. They agree to meet the next day. When Benjamin drives up to Elaine's house the next day, it is raining. Mrs. Robinson, dressed in black, gets in the car, soaking wet. To continue her animal imagery, she is as "mad as a wet hen." She tells Benjamin never to see Elaine again, or she will tell Elaine everything. Benjamin immediately runs out of the car, into the Robinson's house, and up the stairs to Elaine's room.

When Elaine realizes that it is her mother that Benjamin has had an affair with, she screams at him to get out. As he does, Mrs. Robinson leans back against a white wall in her wet, black dress. The camera moves back, and she seems to melt into the whiteness. This scene relates to the scene with Benjamin spiritually drowning in his black diving suit in the pool. Mrs. Robinson, moreover, is also dripping wet; this connects the two scenes and the drowning imagery. It is now Mrs. Robinson who is spiritually drowning and who must continue her death-in-life.

Benjamin is next seen staring into his aquarium, a further extension of the drowning imagery. While he drives to Elaine's and watches her from his car, then watches his father clean the pool, and later watches Elaine in a brown coat leave for college we hear the song "Scarborough Fair/ Canticle." This song comments upon Elaine and Berkeley. The lyrics—"Are you going to Scarborough Fair: . . . . . . Remember me to one who lives there."—tell of Benjamin thinking of going to Berkeley (are you going?) and Elaine (one who lives there) and their relationship. ("Scarborough Fair/ Canticle" © 1966 Paul Simon. Used by Permission.)

Benjamin finally emerges from his death-in-life by making a decision. He will pursue Elaine and marry her. When he makes this decision, he is wearing a brown coat like Elaine's. When he tells his father and mother that he and Elaine are going to be married, his father is in light blue, and his mother wears a white-and-black zebra-striped dress, equating them with the Robinsons and the subculture. When Benjamin's mother is going to call the Robinsons on her white phone, Benjamin tells his parents that Elaine does not know about the marriage yet, and in fact, she doesn't even like him. His father says that the whole idea sounds pretty half-baked. Benjamin says, "No, it's not. It's completely baked." These lines work on two levels, and their use here is well thought out. First, there is the incongruity of the line itself. "Half-baked" means not completely done, or "crazy." When Benjamin says, "it's completely baked," the viewer is surprised and laughs at the incongruity. Second, there is double meaning in the phrase; "completely baked" can mean very crazy, or in terms of Benjamin's usage, sensible and complete. This remark is punctuated when a piece of toast pops out of a toaster. This visually realizes the idea in concrete terms. The toast is done—completely baked. Benjamin knows his own mind and value system and will act on his decision. There has also been considerable heat used in the baking.

When Benjamin arrives on the Berkeley campus, he is wearing white pants and shirt and a brown coat. Elaine is also in a brown coat. The landlord at the rooming house where Benjamin goes to stay is wearing a blue shirt and gray sweater, which visually suggest to the viewer that he adheres to the values of the parents of Benjamin and Elaine.

Benjamin watches Elaine several times. She wears the cool colors blue and green (the influence of her parents' cold subculture), but carries a brown purse. In the background of the campus we see some other colors which indicate there are some who share a different value system. Benjamin, in brown and black, boards a bus that Elaine, also in brown and black (which connects them), is riding (which foreshadows the ending of the film which also shows Benjamin and Elaine on a bus). They go to the zoo, where she is to meet a medical student, Carl Smith, by the monkey house. Smith is wearing brown, but it is a different brown than Benjamin's and Elaine's. Smith also wears a blue shirt with black and blue tie. The brown may equate him in part with Elaine (after all, she is going out with him) and he wears other colors that represent the sterile subculture as well. But I propose another interpretation. After Elaine and Carl go off together, Benjamin watches the monkeys, which are also brown. I think Nichols may want the audience to equate Carl (in the different brown from Benjamin and Elaine) with a monkey. Elaine and Carl were to meet by the monkey house. On the cage containing two monkeys (standing for Elaine and Carl?) there is a sign— "Please do not tease." They also may be making monkeys of themselves, Benjamin in brown included.

Benjamin goes back to his room. Elaine, in a blue sweater and brown coat, comes to visit him in the rooming house. She wants to find out why he is in Berkeley. She learns that her mother lied to her. Mrs. Robinson told Elaine that Benjamin seduced her one night when she was drunk. When Elaine learns the truth about the affair, she is upset. She tells Benjamin that she doesn't want him to leave until he has a definite plan, and she leaves. Later that night, with the light through the windows in Benjamin's room casting a warm glow, Elaine returns and asks Benjamin to kiss her. He does, a very tender kiss. He asks her to marry him. She says she doesn't know. Then, like a nice girl, Elaine leaves.

In a series of quick scenes shot on various parts of the campus, Benjamin now tries to persuade Elaine to marry him. Elaine continues to wear her brown coat and Benjamin wears a white jacket, white pants, and dark blue shirt. The colors may relate to the ending of the film, where he may not be able to overcome completely his parents' values (I shall discuss this further, later).

While whistling the tune "Mrs. Robinson," Benjamin goes to a jewelry store to buy a ring for Elaine. The clerk is wearing blue. There is a young couple in the store with a child who may visually symbolize Benjamin's hope for the future with Elaine.

Benjamin goes to his room and is surprised to find Mr. Robinson waiting for him. Mr. Robinson is dressed in a white raincoat and black tie. The black and white, as usual, appears to suggest two-dimensionality—the character has lost all depth and has become a cartoon image. Mr. Robinson tells Benjamin that he and Mrs. Robinson are getting a divorce and that he is taking Elaine away where Benjamin cannot get to her. No amount of explaining on Benjamin's part can stop the threats and rage of Mr. Robinson.

Benjamin runs to Elaine's dorm, and a note is brought to him by her roommate, who is appropriately dressed in blue. In the note, she tells Benjamin that although she loves him, it would never work out.

Panicked over the thought of losing Elaine, Benjamin drives to her home in Los Angeles. The melody of "Mrs. Robinson" provides the background rhythm for this scene. Benjamin is still dressed in the white jacket, dark blue shirt, and white pants, an outfit which he will wear until the conclusion of the film.

Benjamin secretly enters her home, goes upstairs, and finds Mrs. Robinson in the bedroom. She is dressed in black and white and carrying a raincoat, which recalls her last meeting with Benjamin in the rain and Mr. Robinson's visit to his room. She icily tells him that she can't invite him to Elaine's wedding and calls the police to report Benjamin as a burglar. "I'll find her," says Benjamin. "I think not," says Mrs. Robinson. Benjamin flees. Elaine has decided to follow her parents' wishes, marry Carl Smith, and do what she feels is best.

To the song "Mrs. Robinson," with the words, "And here's to you Mrs. Robinson, Jesus loves you more than you will know. . . . " Benjamin drives back to Berkeley and to Carl Smith's fraternity. ("Mrs. Robinson" © 1968 Paul Simon. Used by Permission.) The fraternity boys are animal-like. The word "gorilla" is mentioned. This recalls Smith's first appearance at the monkey house. There is even a white dog on the table eating breakfast with the boys.

In the bathroom of the fraternity house, Benjamin learns that Carl, the "make-out king" (which is surprising, because Elaine is not presented as a make-out queen by Nichols), is getting married in a church in Santa Barbara, and Benjamin takes off, as the song "Mrs. Robinson" is heard again.

Benjamin goes to a gas station in Santa Barbara to find out where the church is. He calls the secretary of Carl Smith's father and says that he is the father's brother, Reverend Smith, and that he has forgotten the location of the church where he is to perform the ceremony. This surprises the gas station attendant, as Benjamin certainly does not look like a minister. The attendant says, "Do you need any gas, father?" Benjamin fails to get gas, and as his red car runs out of fuel, a guitar on the soundtrack also slows down.

At this point, an excellent use of visual symbolism is made. Nichols has Robert Surtees, the cinematographer, photograph Benjamin running toward the camera through an extremely long, telescopic lens. This lens flattens depth perspective, so we see Benjamin running toward us, but he doesn't seem to be getting anywhere. Thus the visual symbolic statement is made through the use of the long lens. Benjamin is running in place, as in one of those dreams where one runs but does not seem to move.

Benjamin finally arrives at the white church, as the guitar on the soundtrack is strummed to sound like bells. Benjamin climbs the stairs and peers through the glass on the balcony overlooking the ceremony. True to form, the people in the church wear black, white, and gray. Mrs. Robinson is wearing an animal collar to reinforce her animal nature.

Benjamin no longer has the values of the materialistic subculture. He has changed his values, knows what he wants, and communicates this directly to Elaine by crying out in anguish and banging on the church window. In a flash of understanding (by the way, after she has repeated the vows with Carl), Elaine answers with an animal-like scream of "Ben," and rushes to him. Mrs. Robinson shouts, "It's too late." Elaine cries, "But not for me." During some screenings, audiences have cheered at this point. As Benjamin fights his way to Elaine, the lighting casts a pinkish hue. Benjamin blocks the door with a huge crucifix (which recalls vampire pictures where the hero fights off evil with a cross), and he leads Elaine to a bus. The bus is appropriately bright orange, a very warm color. They board the bus and sit in the back. As they sit next to each other, the song "The Sound of Silence" is heard. Benjamin and Elaine don't speak to each other. Then the bus moves off, and the camera, placed behind it, shows Benjamin and Elaine through the back windows as the bus moves down the road of life. Elaine is in her white wedding dress and Benjamin, in his dark blue shirt, is holding his white jacket. The colors relate to the underlying meaning of the scene. Benjamin and Elaine are dressed in the cool colors of their parents' subculture. The sound track is playing, "Hello darkness my old friend." The film ends on a slightly depressing note.

Some feel that Benjamin and Elaine will carve out an entirely different life from that of their parents. Others feel that they will be like their parents in a few years. When asked about his interpretation, Nichols said, "In my mind, it's always been that in five miles she's going to say, 'My God, I haven't got any clothes.' "[2]

Of course, in the film, it was not indicated *how* Benjamin and Elaine's lifestyle would be different from their parents'. When Benjamin finally does get Elaine, they both still must live in the world. We assume they will listen to each other and be true to their own values, but what *are* those values?

From the film itself, and certainly from viewing Nichols' six films as a whole, the ending is not ambiguous. There is a strain of sadness throughout *The Graduate* which Bosley Crowther noted.[3] The repetition of "The Sound of Silence" and especially the color symbolism of Benjamin and Elaine's clothes (even though they are in an orange bus) confirm that although there has been change, there has not been enough change.

Nichols' *The Graduate* has been very popular with all age levels. One reason for this is that it is a very accessible film, based on comic forms familiar to most people's experience. Nichols combines three familiar comic structures in *The Graduate*.[4]

First, Nichols uses the familiar plot of young lovers finally marrying despite the obstacles (within themselves and external) to their union. Boy meets girl; boy loses girl; boy gets girl. Second, Nichols uses the convention of a central figure who eventually discovers an error he has been committing in the course of his life. He discovers this error and acts upon his discovery. Finally, Nichols uses riffing, where he takes an initial situation and then runs off a series of gags that revolve around this situation. A good example is Miss De-Witte's reference to Benjamin as Mr. Braniff when he and Elaine are in the hotel, a situation that was set up long before when Benjamin first came to the hotel for his affair with Mrs. Robinson.

Another reason for the film's popularity is that the theme is agreeable to both young and old. The young may like the film for the position it takes on honesty and on acting on one's own beliefs. Stanley Kauffman has said, "Benjamin is neither a laggard nor a lecher; he is, in the healthiest sense, a moralist—he wants to know the value of what he is doing."[5]

The old may like the film for different reasons. John Russell Taylor argues that *The Graduate* is an update of Andy Hardy movies, and that all the older generation's negative and positive values are reinforced.[6] I think he means here that Benjamin rejects "adulterous and alcoholic" (negative values) Mrs. Robinson and wants to "marry" a "nice girl" who doesn't sleep with him (positive values). Mrs. Robinson, guilt-ridden, tries to stop "true love" (positive value) and is punished for her "bad" behavior by losing her husband and her daughter. Even Benjamin and Elaine may not "live happily ever after" because of Benjamin's "bad" behavior with Mrs. Robinson (the old American "evil must be punished" concept). Some people may perceive the film in this way and, therefore, like it.

But the ending suggests a clouded future for Benjamin, not because he has "sinned," but because Nichols may believe, as is shown in all his pictures, that one is trapped by his past culture. He cannot break out; he can only achieve understanding and be true to his own values.

The Graduate is not a heavy protest film like *Getting Straight* or *The Strawberry Statement*. Nor should Nichols be criticized for not going far enough into protest. Nichols' concern is not with destroying a materialistic society where people use each other as objects, but with a young man who questions this value system, decides what is important to him, and acts upon it honestly. This film is about

Benjamin and what happens to him. Benjamin begins as part of the materialistic society, but what makes him different, and prepares the audience for his eventual attempt to change, is his honesty. He is looking for honest values in a corrupt, materialistic society. As Hollis Alpert puts it, "The most important thing in common between Elaine and Benjamin is that they share the urge to see honestly and clearly."[7]

The point Nichols may be making is that Benjamin cannot free himself from the society completely; he can only try, by understanding and being true to himself and his own vision. That he cannot free himself makes *The Graduate* a true tragedy. This is consistent with a vision of the world that I find in all Nichols' films.

Certainly, *Who'a Afraid of Virginia Woolf?* is similar, in that George cannot go on with his existing lifestyle and chooses to destroy the fantasies that are an integral part of his relationship with Martha. George and Martha may not be able to change completely or free themselves entirely from old patterns, but at least they have changed somewhat and know the truth.

The Graduate's popularity may also be due to the way Nichols handled the very volatile theme of a man having relationships with both a mother and daughter. Although Benjamin is aggressive with both women, Mrs. Robinson is shown clearly as the initiator of the affair, and it is clear that she and Benjamin have sex over a long period of time. Elaine is shown as warm and tender, but her romancing with Benjamin in the film is limited to a few kisses. She even leaves the room after he suggests marriage. Perhaps to make the issue of being a lover to both mother and daughter less inflammatory and the film more palatable to audiences in 1967, Nichols concentrated on the sexual nature of Mrs. Robinson and the affectionate nature of Elaine.

Elaine leaves with Benjamin after she has said her vows with Carl, which is a major change from the book, where she leaves before she has said her vows.[8] Nichols made this change, I feel, to suggest that marriage is merely a formality. According to Alpert, "We now see clearly Mrs. Robinson's tragedy, that she was unable to break out of the hollow formality, the prosperous smothering of her own marriage."[9]

Morality is equated with honesty and true love, which win out even after the ceremony is completed. The marriage between Elaine and Carl is not consummated in novel or film.

Nichols creates a coherent universe in *The Graduate*. A close reading of the film in a psychoanalytic frame of reference reveals that the characters' motivations are believable. For example, Benjamin is hurt and angry at being treated as an object. His rage at his parents for treating him as they do and at his symbolic drowning in the pool may be part of his motivation for calling Mrs. Robinson. Note that Benjamin's mother has the same hair style as Mrs. Robinson, and occasionally wears animal clothing (the zebra-striped dress). His father looks like Mr. Robinson. So, Benjamin may live out his rage against his parents by "screwing" the Robinsons, who stand for his parents in his mind. Mrs. Robinson loses her husband and her daughter. Mr. Robinson asks Benjamin, "Do you have a particular hatred for me?" He has lost his wife and daughter and has been cuckolded in the bargain. Surely his business partnership with Benjamin's father will be affected. Benjamin's rage can clearly be seen against Elaine in the strip joint, where he feels sorry and better after he vents it. It can be seen when he calls Mrs. Robinson a broken-down alcoholic. It can be seen where he makes a shambles of the marriage ceremony, even throwing Mr. Robinson against a wall. No wonder he sits quietly on the bus. His rage has been spent and that may be all that is changed.

Rage motivates many characters in Nichols' films. But *The Graduate* is not so much about rage as it is about a man graduating into life and going after what he believes in. This graduation, or emergence, is what is concentrated on through complex visual symbolism. For example, consider the idea that Benjamin is trapped in the materialistic subculture and trying to break out. Nichols shows us this by the use of a glass motif. Benjamin is usually trapped behind some kind of glass. We see him coming through glass doors at the airport. He stares at a diver in the glass aquarium. He calls Mrs. Robinson from a phone booth, where he is seen behind glass. He and Mrs. Robinson are seen in a glass table top. He stares from his raft, eyes behind sunglasses. He removes his glasses when Elaine cries. At the conclusion of the film, Benjamin is behind glass at the church and then locks the representatives of the materialistic subculture in their own church-aquarium with a gold cross as he and Elaine escape. The final shot questions that escape, as we see Elaine and Benjamin behind glass windows in the back of the bus.

So Nichols parallels Benjamin's emergence and change with visual symbols on the screen. We have mentioned water, glass, color, and music as elements of this symbol system. But the bright red sports car has not been commented upon fully, and it may seem like an incongruity that the car is red (the passionate color that suggests sex), even though it is a product of the environment which is primarily sterile and shown in cold colors.

What more appropriate color than red for the society that invests its passion in objects rather than in humans? The status symbol of that society at the time was the car, so it is the color red, certainly not pink. And notice that Benjamin needs the car for transportation and that it runs out of gas (becomes as useless as the subculture). Benjamin is on his own as he runs to the church. He and Elaine finally leave, not in a fancy car, but on the bus, a common mode of transportation.

The Graduate contains the elements of style that are found in other Nichols films. Among these are the many long, continuous takes in which characters talk to each other (reminiscent of Nichols and May skits) and the motif of water which runs symbolically through the film. The environment reflects the characters' state of mind. The film has an angry major male figure who is searching for something, in this case Benjamin searching for an alternative to his parents' values. It has a destructive woman who interacts with the male, in this instance Mrs. Robinson. It has a sterile, often hostile environment. Los Angeles and the neighborhood where Benjamin lives are shown in this way. The characters are upper middle class and educated; part of the action takes place on a college campus. There is a turning point in the film where the main male character changes, makes a decision, and moves to another psychological state. For Benjamin the turning point comes when he decides to pursue Elaine and marry her. Religion does not seem to be a major force in the characters' lives.

The idea that sex and love are separated, with sex destructive and love constructive, appears in the film. Coupled with this is the notion that a truly loving, sexual relationship is not possible. And finally, there is the sad, pessimistic ending where the male character has gained understanding, but not true freedom.

The Graduate is, in my opinion, a masterpiece. All the elements of the symbol system relate to the "spine" of the work. Form and content are perfectly matched.

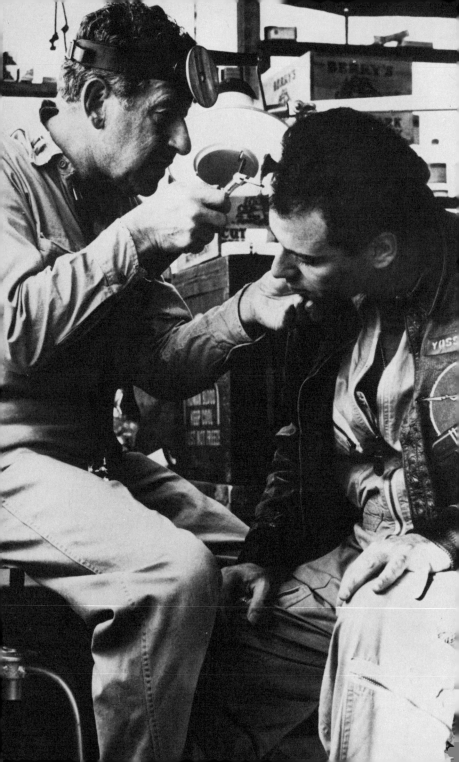

4

Catch-22

Catch-22 is Mike Nichols' third film. It is based on the best-selling book by Joseph Heller, which was originally published in 1962. The cost of the film was over fourteen million dollars.[1]

The story is about an airfield near Italy during World War II. Nichols describes the film not as a literal rendering of what happened during the war but "a dream." He says that the theme is ". . . about when you get off. At what point do you draw the line beyond which you won't go."[2] Captain Yossarian, the protagonist and the one who has the dream, sees the war and army life as mad. Yossarian's predicament is how to deal with what he perceives as the insanity around him. He arrives at wisdom by accepting and understanding his own experience. The film is Yossarian's dream, actually a series of dream sequences, through which Yossarian eventually gains insight.

A useful frame of reference for an analysis of Catch-22 is psychoanalysis. Nichols said, "You must understand that Catch-22 is about a character blocking out a traumatic event, coming in contact with it, and finally collapsing as a result—just like the classical analysis of an hysterical psychoanalytic situation—and coming out of it able to make a decision."[3]

What Yossarian is blocking out is the death of Snowden, a gunner in his plane. Snowden dies of a massive wound as Yossarian tries to help and comfort him. Five times during the film Yossarian remembers this death and the episode is repeated on the screen. But each time, a little more is revealed as Yossarian is able to remember more and more. "Everything Yossarian does," said Nichols, "is because of and about Snowden. . . . As in a psychoanalysis, Yossarian keeps getting closer to a memory and then forgetting it and cutting it off. That's what the movie is. He does not remember the end of Snowden, and he is trying to and it gets cut off. When he does fully

65

remember Snowden, he breaks down and is reconstituted and makes his decision. It is exactly a parallel to psychoanalysis."[4]

The structure of the film allows us to be in Yossarian's mind, and live and relive with him through his dream-rememberings the incidents that bear on his final decision to leave the base and try to escape to freedom. The film is circular in design, with Snowden's death the "spine." This circular pattern is particularly important to the theme of self-discovery—the viewer perceives the full nature of the Snowden event just as Yossarian perceives it. Nichols, in the same article as noted above, explained why he gave his film this circular structure. "The first thing I knew and I told Buck, [Buck Henry, who wrote the film with Nichols] was that the important thing in the book should be the important thing in the movie; and that is going around in a circle, coming back to Snowden over and over again, with each scene a little longer. The movie had to be a circle." The circular nature of the film is also strengthened by the dialogue, which, according to Buck Henry, "keeps going around and around in that maddeningly sophist way."[5] Certain situations are repeated. The chronological sequence of events is jumbled by Nichols for thematic reasons.

Because of the circular design of the film, an analysis of the scenes is imperative for a complete understanding of the brilliant way Nichols has used the filmic symbol system. Henry said, "Everything in the film except the last scene where Yossarian leaves the hospital and goes to Sweden is inside Yossarian's mind."[6] The film thus seems to make more sense if seen as diagramed below:

(See Illustration #1)

This diagram illustrates my speculations on the objective-subjective structure of the film. Thus, the opening credits with dawn breaking over the base, planes taking off, and Yossarian being stabbed (seen for the first time), take place in reality or the outer world. The stabbing motivates the dreaming, as Yossarian dreams while he is unconscious from the wound. All the scenes from the first through the fifth Snowden dream take place in Yossarian's mind, or the inner world. The final scenes of the film, when Yossarian is in the hospital and then in the raft, are again in reality or the outer world. In the outer world, time moves chronologically. In the inner world, time moves psychologically, by non-chronological associations. All the events in the inner world have a bearing on Yossarian's finally remembering what happened to Snowden, and those events also bear on his final decision to try to escape.

ILLUSTRATION NO. 1

Opening Credits
Planes Take Off
Yossarian Stabbed (shown for the first time))   OUTER WORLD REALITY

FIRST SNOWDEN DREAM

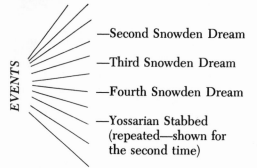

EVENTS

—Second Snowden Dream

—Third Snowden Dream

—Fourth Snowden Dream

—Yossarian Stabbed
(repeated—shown for
the second time)

INNER
WORLD—
YOSSARIAN'S
MIND—
DREAMS

FIFTH SNOWDEN DREAM

Yossarian in Hospital
Yossarian in Raft
Closing Credits)   OUTER WORLD REALITY

The viewer sees Doc from Yossarian's point of view as he climbs into the plane (top). Prepared to take off in *Dumbo* (bottom).

By using an outer-world and inner-world technique, Nichols was able to translate the intention of the book to the screen very successfully.[7] In translating a novel as long and complex as *Catch-22*, Nichols had to shorten and condense. He dropped many characters completely. He concentrated on those directly related to the death of Snowden and Yossarian's problem. He expanded the roles of other characters. Nichols has made Yossarian even more central to the narrative. The inner world is exclusively that of his point of view. Although Yossarian is the center in the novel, the story is told in the third person. It is not Yossarian's interpretation of events, but Heller's, which gives us a total view of an upside-down world. In almost all of the film, events occur only in the inner world of Yossarian. By concentrating on the character of Yossarian, and what the characters and events mean to him, Nichols has narrowed the focus and has created a unified statement and a world very true to itself.

When seen as Yossarian's view of events, many of the departures from reality are understandable. Of course, the General's Wac is a caricature of those sexy starlets from the 1940s, and she is indeed overdrawn. But Yossarian sees her this way, so it is not incongruous to the world created in the film. Obviously, parents of a dying soldier would recognize that Yossarian had taken his place in the hospital (Yossarian was asked by Doc to assume the role of a soldier who had already died in order to not disappoint the man's parents who had come from the States to be with him as he was dying); in fact, Heller tried to make this scene believable by placing it in shadows. But Nichols films this scene in full illumination, for this is how Yossarian interprets it. Please keep the outer world-inner world contrast in mind as I analyze the film's scenes.

The first scene, in the outer world, begins in black and, through it, the credits are superimposed in white. It is dawn. A dog barks. Birds chirp. The viewer sees a valley between two ridges. As the credits end, the sun rises. There is no music, just natural sounds. Suddenly, the tranquility is broken by the sound of engines roaring to life. There are cuts to planes revving their engines, spitting out smoke and fumes. Several planes are photographed in extreme close-up, making them look like monsters. Nichols is showing us that these intruders are polluting this peaceful place. He shows many planes preparing to take off.

Next, also in the outer world, Yossarian is talking with Colonel

Cathcart and Colonel Korn in the ruins of a building. The scene is filmed in long shot, so the ruins are prominent. They are visual comments on the terrible situation facing Yossarian. Since the camera is far back, the noise of the engines purposely drowns out what the men are saying. Yossarian shakes hands with the Colonels, walks out of the ruins, and is stabbed by what looks like a soldier in green. This scene happens again later, but it is shown here as a frame to provide a link to Snowden's death scene and begin Yossarian's dream, or psychoanalysis. After Yossarian is stabbed, the screen goes white, and we are now in the inner world of Yossarian.

The dream about Snowden is a bit overexposed; this suggests that it is somewhat unreal and, therefore, part of the subjective world of Yossarian's mind. It progresses only to the point where Yossarian sees the wounded Snowden. Yossarian has been wounded in the outer world, which motivates the dream about Snowden also being wounded. The idea of dying connects Yossarian and Snowden. (The entire Snowden dream which Yossarian is trying to remember begins when he is in his plane, and he is asked over the headset to help the bombardier. "I'm the bombardier," Yossarian answers. "Then help him, help *him,* " says the voice. Yossarian discovers that the new gunner, Snowden (a symbolic name for purity) has been wounded. Yossarian tries to comfort him. Yossarian looks for morphine, but finds instead a share of M and M Enterprises, another officer's moneymaking scheme. He thinks that Snowden has a superficial wound, but when he pulls back the uniform, he sees that it is a big one. Snowden's insides pour out in Yossarian's hands, and then he covers Snowden's head with a white sheet.)

After the first Snowden dream, a Red Cross unit picks Yossarian up, probably after his knifing. Next, in a mess hall, Yossarian envisions himself being called crazy by some soldiers. In the next scene, Yossarian talks to Doc Daneeka about Catch-22. Yossarian wants to get out of combat missions, so he decides to go crazy. Doc, the flight surgeon, says that he has to ground anyone who is crazy; all one has to do is ask. "And then you can ground him?" Yossarian asks. "No, then I can't ground him. Catch-22. Anyone who wants to get out of combat duty isn't really crazy." So Yossarian's plight is clear; if one is crazy, one has to be grounded, but if one asks to be grounded, then one isn't really crazy. And the impossible situation is that Yossarian still has to fly the missions, and the number of missions he has to fly keeps being increased. Contradictory messages like these are seen throughout *Catch-22*, and the viewer follows Yossarian as he confronts them.

As Yossarian talks with Doc in this scene, they walk to the planes. Many trucks and planes are moving around, but, as in a dream, no people are seen driving or piloting them. This eerie effect is designed to provide the viewer with a clue to Yossarian's psychological state. The viewer knows that he or she is in Yossarian's mind, for as Yossarian hangs upside down when getting into his plane and says good-bye to Doc, the camera is also upside down; the viewer sees Doc upside down from Yossarian's point of view.

In the next scene the planes are ready to take off. Here pilots are flying them, but instead of giving the thumbs up sign as others do, Yossarian gives the finger, which indicates how he feels about the mission. As the planes take off, they are photographed through a long lens, which flattens depth perspective. Thus, as the planes move toward the camera, they seem to be bumping into one another. The action remains on the field, where Milo Minderbinder and Colonel Cathcart talk. Milo, whose name is symbolic like the other names in the film (Minderbinder suggesting that he binds men's minds with his schemes), is introduced to the viewer as he holds up an egg close to the camera. This is a nice visual statement and a good use of the wide screen. The egg, of course, represents one of the commodities that Milo will trade for other commodities and money; thus it is focused on to show that his schemes are his all-consuming passion and will soon dominate the base. Also, we find out subsequently that this scheme is not good, or "lays an egg." Finally, Milo is responsible for the bombing of the base by the Americans (a trade-off with the Germans) and lays eggs of another kind on his own men. Milo is a symbol of those who value money more than human life.

As Milo and Cathcart talk, a plane in trouble tries to land on the runway and crashes. Milo and Cathcart are oblivious to this gigantic crash and loss of life.

Yossarian is next seen in his plane. He is without a parachute because Milo, more interested in dollars than in men's lives, has taken the silk from the chutes to trade. Yossarian is wounded in the leg, and the second Snowden sequence begins. Note that the first Snowden sequence began after Yossarian had been stabbed, so Snowden's death was linked with Yossarian's possible death from the knife wound. Now the second Snowden sequence begins after

Yossarian is wounded by enemy gunfire, again linking the two deaths.

The second Snowden sequence merges with a dream of a nurse in white on a raft. Yossarian is in the ocean swimming toward her. She takes off her white uniform and throws it to him. As he grabs for it, he sinks into the water. It looks as if he is drowning. Yossarian shares the image of symbolic drowning that we have seen with George in *Who's Afraid of Virginia Woolf?* and Benjamin in *The Graduate.* For Yossarian, more than with any character in Nichols' films, the drowning motif is ever present. Yossarian is a bombardier. If his plane is shot down, it will crash into the ocean and he will drown. He is symbolically drowning in the non-humanness about him as well and must save himself.

Yossarian is next seen in the hospital and talks with Chaplain Trappman (this name may have anti-religious implication). Here he sees a man completely covered in white bandages except for his mouth; nurses indifferently change bottles attached to the man while they discuss recipes. As Yossarian screams, there is a cut to Major Major accidentally dropping laundry from a stairway onto a jeep occupied by Colonel Cathcart and Colonel Korn. In the comic routine that follows this scene, Major Major tells Sergeant Towser that he will see people only in his office, but only when he is not in his office (a perfect "catch" situation). In his office, a picture of Roosevelt is seen on the wall. It becomes a picture of Churchill and then Stalin in the same scene. This emphasizes that the scene is taking place in Yossarian's mind. The chaplain, who (of course) cannot get to see the Major, goes to tell Yossarian. Here begins a brilliant linking of scenes with character movement. Korn sees the chaplain talking to Yossarian and takes the chaplain in a jeep to see Cathcart. The chaplain is stopped by Milo, who has a conversation with him. The chaplain then goes to Colonel Cathcart's waiting room and sees Orr, a pilot who tells him that crashing his planes is "good practice." The chaplain then sees Cathcart who (getting off the john) tells the chaplain that he wants some "snappy prayers to make the men feel good," especially so he can get written up in a magazine in the States. Then, as the chaplain leaves, Korn enters, and he and Cathcart discuss their anger toward Yossarian's behavior. "Kick him in the balls," says Cathcart, and there is a cut to a scene where Nurse Duckett (from the dream on the raft) kicks Yossarian in the balls as he tries to make love to her. So Nichols has connected six scenes together with the use of the chaplain's move-² ment. The cut to Yossarian and the nurse ends the sequence, and the transition is motivated by words in one scene being followed by the action these words call for in the next scene.

The next scene introduces General Dreedle, his Wac, and his son-in-law and is played broadly for laughs, again letting us see them as Yossarian does. The following scene takes place in the city where Yossarian first sees Luciana to the strains of Richard Strauss's "Thus Spake Zarathustra," which was also used in Stanley Kubrick's *2001* (1968). Nichols must have known he was borrowing it, and it serves a symbolic function. Here it marks "the beginning" for Yossarian, just as it marked the beginning for the ape men in *2001*. (Other music in *Catch-22* comes from logical sources, such as a radio and a military band.) Luciana is dressed in white, as was the nurse in the drowning scene. The white suggests Yossarian sees them as "ideal" women. The next scene shows Dreedle going to present medals to the men who were going to bomb Ferrara, a harmless civilian town. Yossarian dropped the bombs on the water instead of on the town. He is taking a stand for what he believes in—human life. During the scene of the mission, Yossarian asks, "What the hell are we doing?" Nately replies, "It's not our business to ask." Yossarian says, "Whose business is it?" and then chooses to drop the bombs on the water.

Dreedle, to save embarrassment to the company's reputation, presents a medal to a naked Yossarian (his clothes are in the laundry, covered with Snowden's blood) for a nice tight bombing pattern.

In the next scene, Yossarian is trying to give Luciana the medal ("for killing fish," he says). As they dance in a room, Nichols has the camera revolve in a 360° pan, following them. In a "360," the camera focuses upon something and then moves in a complete circle, ending up where it started. There is a notion in Hollywood that a director has "arrived" when he can use a "360" in a film. The "360" must be motivated by the story and cannot be used arbitrarily. Certainly Nichols used this "360" well. The camera and couple seem to be on a revolving platform. The platform turns, while the camera is focused on the couple as they also turn in the dance. This circular movement is also tied in with the circular design of the film, and this scene motivates still another return to Snowden's death. The strong emotions Yossarian feels with Luciana connect to the strong emotions he feels about Snowden's death, and there is a logical progression from the dance to the death scene.

In this Snowden scene, Yossarian finds that Milo has taken the morphine from the first aid kit and has substituted a share of stock in his M and M Enterprises. The attack on the concept of money being more important than human lives increases. At the end of this Snowden scene, Yossarian screams, "Milo." The next scene takes place on a beach where Milo answers, "Yossarian." It is a fine transition.

McWatt, a pilot, flies across the beach with his plane and cuts in half a soldier standing on a raft. He then flies his plane into a mountain. Sergeant Towser's reply to the death of the soldier who has been cut in half is, "We'll have to requisition a new photographer." The job comes well before the man. Doc is listed as being in the plane, but he is really on the beach watching. Even those who see him standing on the beach believe he has been killed because he is listed in the manifest.

After these deaths, the next scene is, appropriately, a funeral. It is Snowden's funeral, and Yossarian is sitting in a tree, naked, watching it. I feel he is naked for two reasons. First, his clothes may still have not come back from the laundry, but more important, Yossarian and his feelings are "stripped bare." Yossarian has been deeply influenced both by Snowden's death and by Milo's rise to power at the expense of human life. And in this scene, Yossarian can understand that Snowden is dead and that Milo, who stands for so much evil, is alive and well and will continue to grow. Milo suggests to Yossarian some chocolate covered cotton he has invented (he has been stuck with a huge load of cotton in trade). He does not comprehend or care about Snowden's death. Yossarian says, "He got killed." This statement has no meaning for Milo. Nichols brings Snowden and Milo together in this scene, and it is a powerful scene indeed. Yossarian moves closer to drawing the line. Yossarian repeats, "He got killed."

Next there is a cut to Luciana in bed with Yossarian. Luciana says, "What?" and Yossarian says, "I said he got killed." The scene between Yossarian and Luciana is tender and warm and prepares the viewer for the next scene which is a quiet talk between Nately and an old Italian. This is a very moving scene. A number of critics have pointed out that the old Italian spoke with a French accent. In a dream, this would not matter. However, the actor, Marcel Dalio, did appear in the great anti-war film of 1937, *Grand Illusion*, by Jean Renoir, and this link between the two films is a nice gesture by Nichols even if the audience misses it. The Italian argues that Italy will survive because it is weak and America (and perhaps the twenty-year-old Nately) may not survive because it is strong.

In the next scene, the flight back, Milo circles over Orr's crashed and floating plane and tells Yossarian and the other men to stay away from the airstrip that night. As Milo's plane circles, complementing the circular design of the film, Yossarian remembers a conversation with Orr. The next scene finds Yossarian looking for Orr in the empty mess hall. Dance music is playing on the radio or from a phonograph. It is one of the few times music is heard in the film. The lack of music adds to the film's starkness and dreamlike quality. This particular piece of music is also used in Nichols' next film, *Carnal Knowledge*. It establishes the forties period in *Carnal Knowledge* as it relates to the forties in *Catch-22*. It also establishes a link between two films made by the same artist. Note that Nichols' vision embraces the twenties (*The Fortune*), the forties (*Catch-22* and part of *Carnal Knowledge*), the sixties (*The Graduate, Who's Afraid of Virginia Woolf?* and part of *Carnal Knowledge*), and the seventies (*Day of the Dolphin*, part of *Carnal Knowledge*, and the "Family" television series). His skits with Elaine May cover the fifties quite well.

Yossarian says, "Orr?" and there is a cut to the next scene where Doc says, "He's dead," referring not to Orr but to a soldier who has died before his family could visit him. Doc asks Yossarian to pretend he is the soldier for the benefit of the soldier's family who is now at the base. Yossarian does this, partly to get a pass from Doc. After the soldier's family leaves, Yossarian has another vision of Snowden's death. The soldier's death triggers the Snowden dream, with death again linking the two scenes. In the Snowden dream, Yossarian puts a tourniquet on Snowden, and then notices Snowden's big wound.

In the next scene, Yossarian and Nately try to stop Dobbs from killing Colonel Cathcart. The base is bombed. Realizing that Milo and Cathcart have agreed to have their own men bomb their own field in Milo's trade agreement with the enemy, Yossarian tries to shoot Cathcart. His gun is empty.

The next scene finds Yossarian in the operating room. The doctors tell him they are going to clean him out. The camera is from Yossarian's point of view as he lies on the operating table and is looking up as the doctors huddle around. A man in a dark suit leans over and says, "We've got your pal." I assume that, in Yossarian's nightmare, the fellow leaning over is death himself, and the pal he is referring to is Nately, who was killed in the bombing of the base. The killing of Nately provides the motivation for Yossarian to seek out Nately's whore in the city and tell her of his death. Now many painful events, bearing on Yossarian's final decision, take place. The next scenes are examples of some of those events.

Looking for Nately's whore, Yossarian finds that the whores have been rounded up. "Catch-22," an old woman says, is the reason the M.P.'s gave when taking them. He sees Milo riding through the streets looking like Hitler. He is standing in a jeep riding through the crowds in a scene that looks as if it was borrowed from a Leni Riefenstahl German propaganda film. Milo takes Yossarian to a house of prostitution run by M and M Enterprises. Here he finds Luciana, working for Milo as a madam. "Everyone works for Milo," she says. In the house of prostitution, Nately's whore attacks Yossarian when she learns of Nately's death, figuring that Yossarian is in some way responsible. And one of the points of the film is that by doing nothing Yossarian *is* partly responsible, and the motivation of Nately's whore makes sense. Yossarian escapes her and walks through the dark streets of the city, seeing many horrors.

Although this walk has been compared to scenes from Fellini, one of Nichols' favorite directors, much of it comes from the book. The camera concentrates on Yossarian walking while the horrors are shown in the background. It is if Yossarian were walking through hell, and these scenes have a cumulative effect on his final decision.

Yossarian finds that Aarfy (his animalistic name suggesting a dog, or his full name, Aardvark, meaning anteater) has raped a woman "only once" and then killed her so she wouldn't say bad things about him. Yossarian believes Aarfy will be arrested, but it is Yossarian who is arrested for being out past curfew. Nothing seems to happen to Aarfy. The next scene is a repeat of the opening of the film where Yossarian, Cathcart, and Korn are talking in the destroyed building, bombed by American planes. This time the camera is close up instead of far away, and Cathcart and Korn are heard distinctly. They offer Yossarian the choice of a court-martial for desertion or a trip home. If he chooses to go home, he must say nice things about

Cathcart and Korn during the parades and gatherings in his honor. Yossarian decides to accept the offer of going back to the States and shakes hands with Cathcart. As he walks away, Nately's whore, disguised as a soldier, stabs him, but in this shot, she can be recognized by her voice. Everything in the film coalesces now. He recognizes who his assailant is, which leads to the last Snowden scene, which leads to reality. He achieves a double recognition here. In the last Snowden death scene, Yossarian pulls aside Snowden's uniform, sees his insides oozing out, and understands the meaning of his death.

The film now shifts from inner reality to outer reality. The next scene is played in long shot without a cut. It is in the hospital. Yossarian is stretched out dressed in white. His position reminds us of a character we saw earlier—the man completely covered by bandages. Yossarian is immobile. He may be likened to Jesus Christ on the cross. Yossarian learns from the chaplain and Major Danby that Orr has in fact rowed to Sweden. Orr is the pilot who had been practicing crash landings in the ocean. (Note the constant symbolic meanings of the names—for example, one rows with an oar.)

Yossarian, who now fully understands the meaning of Snowden's death, can now make a decision. He decides that he, too, can escape. He will not accept a court-martial or safety in the States. Instead he chooses his own way out. He is not a coward. He just draws the line. There is a cut as he jumps out the window, an act filmed in slow motion, and begins to run. The chaplain and Danby speak to him and he answers them while he is running. Of course, this is not possible in the real world, but in the filmic world Nichols created, it works perfectly. Perhaps we are even back in Yossarian's mind, although this time he is not dreaming. No voices get softer or louder, but the conversation is carried on by cutting back and forth between Yossarian and the two men watching him running away from them. Yossarian jumps into a yellow rubber raft, "The Stars and Stripes Forever" is heard on the soundtrack, and he rows his yellow raft away from the shore and towards Sweden. The camera pulls back. There is a cut to black and credits roll.

Nichols has designed the film in a way that very successfully exploits the filmic symbol system to convert Heller's fictional episodes into visual images. Also very filmic in intent and execution is the manner in which Nichols shifts between various scenes. These transitions capture various confusions between reality and dream, between sanity and insanity. Nichols' transitions from one scene to another are always carefully motivated. One motif in one scene triggers the motif in the next scene. There are visual or audial cues, or both, that link some scenes together. For example, when Yossarian screams after the nurses have callously changed the bottles on the man completely bandaged in white, there is a quick cut to Major Major dropping laundry, as a reaction to that scream. Another good transition is when Cathcart says, "Kick him in the balls," and in the next scene Nurse Duckett kicks him in the balls. In another scene Yossarian and Nately are in the squad room after General Dreedle's first appearance. Nately and Yossarian are talking about Nately's whore. Nately says, "I love her, I do." There is a cut to Nately and Yossarian in a plaza in the town and Nately concludes, "I really do." Another example is when General Dreedle gives Yossarian a medal and there is a cut to where Yossarian gives the medal to Luciana. So the film is not made up of a series of disconnected scenes, but, as in psychoanalysis and in dreams, there is something in each scene which triggers the next; a reaction to something, a phrase that is lived out or repeated, an object that appears in both, etc.

Many people believed that *Catch-22* was a comedy and believed that comedies ought not to be disturbing or raise important or complex issues. Chuck Thegze, in his brilliant review of *Catch-22* in *Film Quarterly* titled "I See Everything Twice," says of the humor in the film, "Nichols and Henry designed *Catch-22* so that the laughter of the film slowly fades as the horror of the film grows." Thegze reports that Nichols says of the humor that "Catch-22 was *designed* [italics mine] to be funny and then not at all."[8] It is this aspect of the humor that is disquieting. Nichols combines humor and horror. For example, Yossarian receives a medal in the nude, which is funny. But then we learn that the reason he is in the nude is that his uniform is covered with Snowden's blood, which is horrifying.

Catch-22 shares three characteristics which Gerald Mast has described as typical of many contemporary American films.[9] First, the protagonists of the films are social misfits, deviates, or outlaws. The villains are the legal, respectable defenders of society. Certainly in *Catch-22* the villains are indeed the legal defenders (in the Army, no less). Yossarian deviates from this society, even though he is obviously one of the few in the film who is not crazy. Second, the new American cinema does not ask to be taken as a picture of reality, but constantly announces that it is artificial. Certainly the circular, psychoanalytic design of the film, Yossarian's slow-motion jump out the window, and the overexposed Snowden scenes place *Catch-22* in this category. Third, the new films play as trickily with sound as they do with images. In *Catch-22*, Nichols manipulates the sound symbols cleverly. The music from *2001* heard as Yossarian sees Luciana, the roar of the planes covering conversations, the audial transitions, and Yossarian carrying on a conversation with the chaplain and Danby as he runs are examples of "tricky" but appropriate sound usage.

The Graduate also shares these characteristics to a certain extent. *Who's Afraid of Virginia Woolf?* is more realistic than artificial. It should be noted, however, that all Nichols' films except *Catch-22* move chronologically in time. *Catch-22* moves psychologically, back and forth around a giant circle. Other films that employ a similar style to *Catch-22* are Federico Fellini's *8½* (one of Nichols' favorite films), Richard Lester's *How I Won the War* and *Petulia*, and Alain Resnais' *Hiroshima, Mon Amour*.

One may speculate why Nichols chose to make *Catch-22* at the time he did. For one thing, the war in Viet-Nam was being waged, and *Catch-22*, although set in World War II, certainly made statements and had connotations that applied to Viet-Nam. Few films were produced about Viet-Nam during that war. Several films were produced dealing with war in general. It was safer for producers, who did not wish to offend anyone, and for the viewer as well, I suspect, to have images dealing with present-day feelings set in the past—the Korean War, World War II, or a fictional event. Among recent anti-war films, *Catch-22* may be the most directly relevant to the American experience in Viet-Nam. *How I Won the War* (1967) is not an anti-war movie but an "anti-war-movie" movie. It shows how absurd the images of war are in our patriotic war pictures compared to the reality of war. *M*A*S*H* (1970) reinforced the horrors of war by providing a survival kit to cope with them: keep a sense of humor and one will survive, and even have fun. *Patton* (1970) concerned itself with an old warrior, a noble man out of his time. Even if you disagreed with him, you at least understood him. *The Green Berets* (1968) was one of the fantasy films that *How I Won the War* was parodying. To Nichols' credit, *Catch-22* was the film about war for the seventies, for it said that human life was most important and that one had to draw the line in order to survive and be at peace with oneself.

Seen in this context, Yossarian isn't running away. He could have gone back to the States and done that. He is acting according to his principles; he is drawing the line beyond which he will not go. I imagine that many young men who resisted the Viet-Nam War draft for moral reasons got great comfort from Catch-22.

Yossarian rowing away in his raft is a typical Nichols ending. In the novel, Yossarian takes off toward Rome to hitch a ride to Sweden. Heller says of the ending, "At the end of the movie, Yossarian goes out in the ocean, with a little paddle and a rubber raft, to row to Sweden. That's not in the book, but it's exactly the effect that I tried to create with the ending of the novel."[10] Nichols changed the ending, keeping Heller's intent, but aligning it with his own personal vision. The male character has gained insight and is now trying to save himself. But, can Yossarian really row to Sweden in a little yellow rubber raft? Nichols shows us Yossarian in the raft in long shot with a long way to go even to get away from the base. The ending is optimistic only in that Yossarian has made a decision and has drawn the line. Whether he will gain freedom is doubtful. Like George in Who's Afraid of Virginia Woolf? and Benjamin in The Graduate, he may not make it. But at least all three characters have moved to a new psychological state, have made a decision, and have acted on it.

Yossarian

5

Carnal Knowledge

Carnal Knowledge was released by Avco Embassy in 1971. It was produced and directed by Mike Nichols and written by Jules Feiffer, playwright and famed cartoonist for *The Village Voice*. Unlike Nichols' three previous films, *Carnal Knowledge* was not based on other existing works, but was composed for the screen. Although it has many comic moments, it makes a very serious statement on the contemporary human condition. It traces the lives of two friends from their college days at Amherst in the mid-1940s to their adult years in Manhattan in the early 1970s. (Thus Nichols returns to the same Massachusetts college settings that he used in his first picture.) Jonathan (Jack Nicholson), the main protagonist, is handsome and sexually attractive; Sandy (Arthur Garfunkle), the second protagonist, is less attractive. Both are intelligent.

During the credits (red on black) we hear the voices of Jonathan and Sandy. We also hear dance music of the forties. Jonathan and Sandy discuss love and sex; we learn that they both seem to want the same things from a woman; mutual understanding and sexual gratification. After the credits, another dance tune begins; we see a red car, and then Susan (Candice Bergen), a coed, enters a college dance, alone. She is wearing a black sweater and a black-and-yellow checked skirt with some red. Note the red, a bright color associated with passion, as a continuing design element from the credits into the first scene. The camera follows her in close-up as she moves through the room, as it did when it followed Benjamin in the party scene in *The Graduate*. She passes students Jonathan and Sandy. Sandy wears a gray (a neutral, sexless color) sports coat. Jonathan wears a reddish sports coat. The walls are yellowish white. Jonathan says that he gives Susan to Sandy and advises him to tell her about his unhappy childhood. Sandy walks over and tries to talk with her. In one shot, Susan and Sandy stand together in the foreground, with

85

Jonathan looking on from the side in the background. This shot foretells the future relationship between the characters; with Sandy and Susan together and Jonathan watching in the background.

In the next scene, Jonathan and Sandy are in their dormitory room in their beds. Nichols makes an aesthetically pleasing use of the wide screen here by having the beds at each side of the screen and having dormitory furnishings in the center. They discuss Susan in sexual terms, although we learn from this conversation that Susan combines both sexual and spiritual qualities.

The next scene takes place on the Smith campus. Sandy is trying to kiss Susan. Susan wears black, although in other scenes she wears other colors. Almost all the women wear primarily black in this film, and often black and white. This seems to be because the male characters see women in simplistic terms, as black and white, and not in complex terms. They may also be "evil" and black, at least in Jonathan's mind. In this scene Susan explains that she doesn't let a boy she likes know how smart she is and that she would someday like to write novels. Sandy seems more interested in kissing her and "scoring." After he tries to kiss her, she says. "Don't press so hard." This applies not just to the kiss, but to Sandy's sexual advances toward her.

In the next scene, Jonathan is in the shower in the dormitory. This introduces a motif: Jonathan taking showers. We have seen the motif of water running throughout Nichols' films, and the shower continues that motif. The shower here takes place during sexual talk and showers continue to be associated with sexual talk or activities throughout the film. Jonathan and Sandy discuss Susan in sexual terms, and Sandy agrees to try and feel her up.

In the woods, Sandy and Susan have an argument about sex. When Susan learns that Sandy is a virgin (as she is), she agrees to petting and masturbates him.

Jonathan and Sandy discuss this event on campus in one continuous shot containing camera movement. Dead leaves blow around, signaling fall and creating a pessimistic tone. The dead leaves appear before the marriage ceremony in *The Fortune,* and at the beginning of *Who's Afraid of Virginia Woolf?* Sandy doesn't concentrate on the warm feeling and mutual understanding that he and Susan shared, but concentrates on the physical and sexual acts. Sandy has on a red-and-black checked coat. The red may indicate the passion in him for Susan.

In fact, Sandy is so gleeful and specific about his sexual relationship with Susan that Jonathan calls Susan and tries to have sex with her. The call from the phone booth is reminiscent of the call Benjamin made to Mrs. Robinson. However, this time it is the man who is interested in sex and the woman who is being seduced.

When Jonathan, wearing gray, meets Susan outside of her sorority house, she is wearing a tan camel coat and a white blouse underneath. Tan instead of black on Susan in this scene may suggest the possibility of a meaningful relationship with Jonathan. Brown shades are also neutral, toned down from red and yellow, and suggestive of convention. They drive to a college town bar. Inside the bar, Nichols has the camera concentrate on Jonathan and Susan in a two shot with Jonathan on one side and Susan on the other. The lighting makes them seem as if they both are wearing brown. Jonathan sets up another date with her. In the dormitory room, Jonathan learns from Sandy that Susan likes Sandy because he is sensitive. This causes Jonathan to tell Susan about his past as they sit in his car. Susan wears a red scarf here, perhaps indicating her growing passion for Jonathan.

What Jonathan says about his father reveals much about his character. He says that his father has been a failure and could not hold onto a job. But he also kept giving Jonathan advice. In a way, this suggests, in part, Jonathan's and Sandy's relationship throughout the years. Jonathan certainly fails, not sexually, but in the quality of his relationships with women. And these relationships are temporary. So as his father cannot hold a job, Jonathan cannot "hold" a woman. In addition, he constantly gives Sandy advice. "The more he failed, the more he gave advice," says Jonathan about his father, and this applies to the advice he gives Sandy even the last time they are together. The payoff of the scene is when Susan says, "You're a lot more serious than I thought." Jonathan says, "I know." This indicates that Jonathan knows all along that he is using the serious talk as a way of seducing Susan, and he had suggested to Sandy that one way to seduce girls is to tell them about an unhappy childhood. It also tells alert viewers, however, that Jonathan *is* much more serious than they realized. It recalls the beginning of the film when he seriously says he does not want to be hurt. The scene also recalls Benjamin and Elaine's serious talk in the car in *The Graduate*.

Outside the library, Jonathan tells Sandy that he has met a terrific girl, but does not tell him that the girl is Susan. Blue, a cold color, predominates. Later, in the dorm room, he says that her name is Myrtle.

In the next scene Jonathan and Susan are having sexual intercourse in the woods. The camera is in close-up and looks down on them. Jonathan is on top of Susan and covered by a fur coat. He looks like an animal. He is groaning. She is gasping and doesn't look as if she is enjoying it. Jonathan rolls off her. Susan sits up quickly and then lies down again. She does not speak. Jonathan looks at her, then up at the sky. He smiles, wolfishly. The sex act is depicted as a brutal act with little loving care on the part of either Jonathan or Susan. Sex and love are certainly separate here.

The next shot is of the gymnasium swimming pool in the morning. Sandy is in the pool. Jonathan jumps in the pool gleefully and indicates that he is no longer a virgin. There was a pool in *The Graduate*, too, where Benjamin drowned symbolically. In a way, Jonathan may also be symbolically drowning here, although he is happy about it. He is celebrating a sexual conquest rather than the completion of a loving relationship. And seeing women solely in sexual terms is indeed part of his later living death.

In the locker room, Sandy tells Jonathan that it is now his turn. Jonathan asks Sandy not to tell Susan about his sexual conquest. In the dorm room, Sandy tries to have sex with Susan. She says, "Sometimes I want to do it and a second later I don't want to do it." Sandy tells her he loves her. Susan worries whether the condom is safe. So Susan, who loves Sandy, finds it difficult to have sex with him (not just because she may feel guilty about sleeping with both men), although she finally brings herself to do it. Here again, we see the split between sex and love. She can have sex with Jonathan. She cares for Sandy, I feel, and therefore may have trouble having sex with him. A relationship both loving and sexual seems impossible in this film.

On the street, with snow prominently on the ground, Sandy tells Jonathan about making it with Susan. The snow is significant, for Jonathan's relationship with Susan is growing colder, and he himself is heading toward his death-in-life. The next scene finds Jonathan and Sandy with Susan at the college bar. They are dancing to juke box music. (The music in *Carnal Knowledge* comes from logical sources, such as the juke box, a phonograph, etc.) Susan is wearing black. She is dancing first with Sandy, who is very mechanical in his movements. She looks at him with affection. Then she dances with Jonathan and looks at him with lust. The scene is repeated with variations in Nichols' later work, *The Fortune*. Next is a close-up of Susan at a table. Jonathan and Sandy sit on either side of her, but are not seen. Susan laughs and they play word games. The scene lasts quite a long time. It is positioned here, and Susan is held on the screen so long, I feel, for two reasons. One, Susan's face certainly dominates the scene, as she dominates both men's lives. Secondly, she is clearly enjoying herself. She has a complete relationship with the two men; Sandy for love, Jonathan for sex. But she can't enjoy sex and love with the same person, an important point.

Next, on the Smith campus, Jonathan, now in black, tells Susan that this has to stop; she must tell Sandy about their relationship and in effect choose between them. She says she doesn't want to hurt Sandy. Jonathan objects, and I think significantly, that he himself is being hurt. During the rest of his life Jonathan finds it easier to relate to women on sexual, rather than on emotional, terms. If he becomes emotionally involved he fears he will be hurt, as he was with Susan. He also tells her, after a long pause, that he loves her.

In the dormitory room, Sandy and Jonathan talk. She has not told Sandy. In Susan's sorority house, with Susan in the cold color blue, Jonathan tells her to tell Sandy about their relationship. If she refuses, he will tell Sandy. The next scene is moving and significant. There are cuts between Jonathan and Susan on the phone. Both are wearing blue, cold colors. The blue, a major color motif, will be used even more throughout the next part of the film, perhaps indicating the coldness of Jonathan, Sandy, and their relationships with women.

Susan did not tell Sandy about her and Jonathan. Jonathan tells her that he also did not tell Sandy, for he knew that Sandy would run to her and that she would go to bed with him. Here is the key dialogue, as taken from the soundtrack of the film:

JONATHAN: Do you think there's any sense in this?
SUSAN: In what?
JONATHAN: In you and me?
SUSAN: That's up to you.
JONATHAN: No, it's up to you. I don't see any point in it. I wish I were wrong. I don't feel anything anymore.
SUSAN: Neither do I.

Susan tells Jonathan she will always be his friend. Jonathan says, "Jesus, Susan—I hope not."

When Jonathan says he doesn't feel anything any more, I think it is the opposite of what is happening. Indeed he does feel something for Susan. She has hurt him so much that he says he no longer wishes to be her friend. And the feelings of love and trust (he even says he used to trust her) have turned to hurt and anger, so much so that he will consider women in sexual terms from now on. Although he has adopted this policy before somewhat, partly to protect himself from being hurt, he did let himself become emotionally involved with Susan. After his experience with her, he will definitely choose sexual involvement with other women.

After Susan and Jonathan talk on the phone, the next scene shows Susan, in white blouse, and Sandy packing for a trip to the tropics together for a honeymoon, it seems. Jonathan is between the two, but we only see his face in close-up. There is a reddish orange glow to the scene, perhaps indicating Jonathan's passionate anger. Jonathan is not happy. Susan makes fun of Sandy and obviously has the upper hand. As she and Sandy bicker back and forth, Jonathan looks directly at the camera. We hear skating music.

There follows a very significant sequence. To the accompaniment of skating music (organ music as one might hear at a skating rink) the screen bleaches to a passionless white. Jonathan's image disappears. A beautiful woman, dressed in white, is seen skating on ice. This scene represents the changes taking place in Jonathan and in Susan. Overwhelmed by anger (reddish-orange), Jonathan chooses to withdraw from emotional involvement and so in a sense chooses emotional death (ice, the color white). The beautiful woman suggests Jonathan's ideal woman, beautiful, untouched, covered up, skating through life. This is also the kind of woman Susan becomes when she chooses Sandy. The white the skater wears may also relate to Yossarian's images of ideal women, the nurse and Luciana dressed in white, in *Catch-22*.

So the screen fades to white, and the image of the skater appears. It is now the early 1960s. The camera pulls back to show Jonathan and Sandy in New York watching the skater. Jonathan has become a tax lawyer; Sandy, a doctor. They discuss in sexual terms the skater and Jonathan's actress friends. Another woman, Sally Joyce, walks by. We learn that she has been on the Ed Sullivan show and that Jonathan "fucked her once." Two of Jonathan's women are actresses—experts in projecting a glamorous image. For him the image of a woman is more important than the real women. He praises Susan as a jewel. A jewel, significantly, is a hard, glittering substance. It is not soft and warm.

Another aspect of Jonathan's feelings about women is seen clearly when he says, "You think a girl goes for you and you find out she's after your money or your balls; or your money and your balls. The women today are better hung than the men."

The next scene takes place in Sandy's office. As he stares into the camera and talks about his conventional, boring life with Susan, there is the city behind him in blue. Both the dialogue and the visual background suggest that Sandy's relationship with Susan is cold.

The next scene takes place at a restaurant. Jonathan is having dinner with Bobbie (Ann-Margret), a model dressed in black. The camera focuses on them, while the background revolves as in a revolving restaurant. This adds interest to the exposition. Bobbie does television commercials, a profession concentrating on images. She is a lovely, sexy woman. We learn that Bobbie is twenty-nine and that Jonathan is sexually interested in her. In the taxi they joke about marriage. She says that if they were married and then got a divorce, she would take him for every cent he had. He asks if she will take pity on him. She says only if he says he's sorry and will always be a good boy. (This predicts the outcome of their relationship. They marry and get a divorce. But Jonathan can never say he is sorry to a "ball buster" and therefore is killed with alimony.) Back to the taxi; she asks if he likes to be mothered. He tells her he would like to be smothered by her. Perhaps Jonathan secretly would like to be mothered by women, be taken care of, and is afraid of that motivation. But to me, smothered suggests death. When one is smothered, one can't breathe and dies (as when one drowns).

They go to Jonathan's apartment to make love. Nichols then begins a shot on Bobbie's coat and has the camera travel through the apartment into the bedroom, where we see her and Jonathan making love. Just a little light spills from the bathroom. We hear sounds of passion, not tenderness. A record is playing. It is Frank Sinatra singing "Dream." This relates to Jonathan's dream of women, rather than the reality of women. The dim lighting may have been necessary to avoid censorship problems, but it also suggests that Jonathan sees only the sexual side of Bobbie. He does not see her completely, as he would in full light.

The next scene takes place in Jonathan's bedroom during the day.

Classical music is playing. Jonathan is in the shower, and Bobbie is on the bed, naked, eating a snack. It is important to know how much time Bobbie spends in bed and how her relationship with Jonathan is centered around the bed. Here she is eating in bed and reading the paper. They kid around and she joins him in the shower. Jonathan is symbolically drowning in this relationship; thus the shower is indeed appropriate. Next, we see them in bed at night. Bobbie refers to most men as "pricks" but decides that Jonathan is nice. He goes to the shower. There is a long close-up of Bobbie in bed thinking. When he returns she suggests they "shack up." Jonathan sits away from her and is very cautious. In fact, he compares it to a business deal. She says, "You're a real prick, you know that?" Of course, this scene illustrates the lack of love on the part of Jonathan in the relationship. He sees Bobbie only as a sexual partner.

In the next scene, Jonathan and Sandy are in a bar. Jonathan is in close-up looking at the camera although he is talking to Sandy. Smoking his cigar, Jonathan tells Sandy that he could get serious about Bobbie and that he has had trouble "getting hard" in the past, but with Bobbie he didn't. He discusses Bobbie mainly in sexual terms. When Sandy says that looks aren't everything, Jonathan says, "Believe me, looks are everything." This further reinforces the idea that Jonathan is interested in the outer woman, not the inner one. Sandy, still not convinced, says, "Maybe."

Next we see Jonathan and Bobbie in bed. He wants her to quit work so they won't have to eat so late. When she talks about having children he takes a shower. Here the shower takes on the added meaning of interrupting their conversation.

Next we see Bobbie preparing to serve Jonathan his TV dinner in bed. Note again how the relationship centers around the bed. They will even have dinner together in it, and she will *serve* him. The camera follows her from the kitchen, which is also used as a darkroom to develop pictures. On one wall is a giant black-and-white photograph of Bobbie. There is also a different photograph of Bobbie in black and white next to Jonathan by the bed. Apparently, Jonathan has been taking and developing these pictures. Again he is concerned with the two-dimensional image of the woman, not the woman herself. He sees none of her subtleties of emotion and he really doesn't understand her. He does not see her in "full color." Perhaps he is more involved with the photographs than with her.

The photographs are evocative visual symbolism on Nichols' part; they are not in the published script by Feiffer.

Bobbie is in a light blue robe, a cool color. Jonathan is wearing a white shirt and brown pants. He is watching television, and there is an old musical on the screen. Dick Powell is singing "I'll String Along With You." Here is another example of Nichols' symbolic use of a song which comes from a logical source on the screen. The song comments on Jonathan and Bobbie's relationship. He wishes she were an angel, the ideal woman. She is not, but until one comes along, he will stay with her. Also it describes Bobbie's feelings. Jonathan is no angel either, but to her, as she says later, "he's a gift."

Next we see Jonathan and Sandy in Jonathan's living room. Sandy is the one looking at the camera and smoking a cigar now, and this connects with the scene where Jonathan talked to Sandy about Bobbie while smoking a cigar and looking toward the camera. It is as if he wishes to imitate Jonathan and looks up to him. Sandy, still married to Susan, explains that although he and Susan do "all the right things" their lovemaking is boring. And he says, "Maybe it's just not meant to be enjoyable with women you love." Here again we see the split between love and sex, and the virtual impossibility in the world created in Nichols' film for two people to have both a loving and a sexual relationship. It is either one or the other. Jonathan asks Sandy if he wants to get laid. Sandy replies, "Please."

We are now on a tennis court. Sandy's new woman, Cindy, is introduced moving up into the frame holding a tennis racket. It is assumed from the last scene that Jonathan got Cindy for Sandy. She sits with Bobbie on a bench to watch Jonathan and Sandy play tennis. Cindy is dark, sleek, and alert. She wears white. Bobbie is in black and wears a whitish fur coat. She needs the coat for warmth, not only from the weather. She is not getting warmth from Jonathan. Bobbie is reading a copy of *The Ladies' Home Journal.* It is clear here that she is interested in traditional things, like marriage and children. Cindy is competitive and interested in the sport. Jonathan and Sandy ignore Bobbie while asking Cindy what she thinks. Bobbie says that it is her turn to play, but Jonathan tells her that she is so awful. He plays with Cindy while Bobbie just stares. Cindy is winning. She is indeed a "ball-buster," tennis balls and men's balls.

Next we see Jonathan in the shower, which has become a motif in the film. He then joins Bobbie in the bedroom. He bickers with her about a bill. She puts on a black bra and wears black panties and a white robe, continuing the black-and-white symbolism. The phone rings and neither answers it. Seeing that she is upset and has been taking pills, Jonathan comes over and kisses her. She tells Jonathan she wants to get married. She is frightened because she is now sleeping all the time. She thinks that marriage is the answer to her and Jonathan's problems. Jonathan refuses to marry, although he wants her home all the time, to take care of him, to be there when he wants her sexually. She says that she doesn't want a job, just him. Later, he says that if she wants money, he will pay her to clean up the house.

Then:

JONATHAN: Bobbie, you don't need me. Why do you let yourself in for this kind of abuse? Walk out. Leave me! Please leave me, Bobbie. For God's sake, I'd almost marry you if you'd leave me.

BOBBIE: You call that abuse? You don't know what I'm used to. With all your carrying on, to me, you're a gift. So what's it gonna be?

We see here that Bobbie is very emotionally disturbed. In the past she has chosen men that have abused her and no doubt have seen her only as a beautiful body. Also, she sees the only way to happiness is marriage. This, of course, will not solve the problems of the relationship. Jonathan really doesn't understand Bobbie. He sees her as a sexual object. And Bobbie doesn't understand Jonathan. She feels it is *her* problem, that there is something wrong with her. And the film strongly suggests that they really don't understand themselves.

Sandy and Cindy arrive in the midst of the argument, which echoes the arrival of Nick and Honey in *Who's Afraid of Virginia Woolf?* Cindy is dressed in black and white, of course. Some critics think that she is Sandy's second wife, as Susan is not mentioned or seen during the Cindy sequences. I feel that she is his mistress for several reasons. She looks at a record and says, "I (not we) got this at home." Jonathan later says to her, "You're his girl," rather than his *wife*. And finally, when dancing with Jonathan later, she wears no wedding ring. Nichols emphasizes this in a shot where she is holding Jonathan and we see her hands. She does wear rings, but not one on the wedding ring finger.

The couples are supposed to go to a party together. While waiting for Bobbie to get ready, Cindy, like Mrs. Robinson in *The Graduate*, puts on a cha-cha record. Sandy and Jonathan go to the kitchen. We learn that Cindy is competitive, hands out orders in bed, and makes Sandy give her everything she wants. Again Sandy turns Jonathan on by discussing his sexual relations with a woman. Jonathan suggests that he and Sandy switch partners. Sandy agrees. During this conversation, Sandy and Jonathan are in the foreground in the kitchen; in the background, seen in the living room through the hall, is Cindy swaying to the music.

Jonathan approaches Cindy and Sandy goes to the bedroom to find Bobbie. When Jonathan tries to kiss Cindy, she pulls away. But they finally dance. He tries to seduce her, and says that it is all right with Sandy. She says that Jonathan may come around another time. But, she says, if Sandy has sex with Bobbie, he is not to come home. She seems to mean *her* home, not *their* home.

Sandy discovers that Bobbie has taken an overdose of sleeping pills. While waiting for the ambulance he calls Jonathan a bastard. Jonathan bolts from the room. He sees Bobbie's overdose as a manipulative device, forcing him into marriage. "Very slick, very clever," he screams, and "It's not gonna work, Bobbie." He has no idea of what Bobbie has been feeling. The camera has moved with him. He has run to the door, opened it, closed it, and returned. This visually shows that he cannot escape his dilemma.

He is crying and brings his hands to his face. There is a fade to white, and we hear the skater music.

The skater music is seen over a title slide, "Jonathan Fuerst Presents." (Note the symbolic pronounciation: Jonathan *First?*) This is an excellent transition into the seventies. Jonathan is showing slides of his various women to Sandy and Sandy's new young woman, Jennifer. He calls his show "Ball Busters on Parade." He shows slides of the various women in his life and comments on them mainly in sexual terms. The women in the slides wear primarily black and blue (another symbol perhaps; black and blue is the color of a bruise when one has been hurt) and some early slides are completely in black and white. (Even his daughter, Wendy, is in blue in her slide, with red mittens on her hands. Wendy is in a position that resembles Jesus on the cross, complete with red (blood) covered hands. Bobbie, divorced from Jonathan, is shown

wearing a red sweater, perhaps connoting blood rather than passion.)

Jonathan's apartment is white, very cold and harsh. There is a
mirror on the wall with a red frame around it—appropriately, for
Jonathan only loves himself, and the red, a warm passionate color,
surrounds the mirror in which he can see his own image. Jennifer
wears black. Jonathan wears black and white. Sandy wears a red
shirt. This suggests that he may have found love and passion with
Jennifer, but later exposition tends to deny it. Or, it could equate
him with Bobbie and her red sweater, for he also will be hurt by
Jonathan. Jonathan shows a slide of Susan, describing her as his first
fuck, but quickly changes it to the next woman, saying it was a
mistake. He then calls this woman, Eileen, his first fuck. Jonathan
does this not because he thinks of every woman as the first, but
because he wants to spare Sandy's feelings. However, it is not so
much Sandy's feelings about Susan he is worried about, but Sandy's
feelings about Jonathan himself.

After the show, Jennifer cries (I assume she is saddened by
Jonathan and his past) and Sandy stares in horror. They say nothing
and leave.

The horror is not just that Sandy has recognized Susan and has
been hurt. It is also because of the way Jonathan views real women.
The images on the screen suggest that for him they are images, not
real, three-dimensional women. Since he can see women only as
ball-busters and sexual objects, he cannot relate to them and ends
up alone.

In the next scene, Jonathan and Sandy are walking at night. The
lights of the city stare at them. Both are in brown and black. Sandy
tells Jonathan that Jennifer is his love teacher and that he is through
playing games. Jonathan sees her as a "good piece of ass." Jonathan
says, "Sandy, I love you but you're still a shmuck." As they talk,
Sandy walks out of the frame, so there is a shot of Jonathan alone,
then Sandy alone. Sirens are heard in the background, a very good
use of the cinematic symbol system. Jonathan will end up alone, and
we see this visually. The place where Sandy stood next to him is now
empty. The sirens are like a warning that this will happen, that he
will end life alone.

The last scene begins on a close-up of Jonathan as he enters the
apartment of the prostitute Louise. The apartment has a warm feeling, but Louise wears some black and white. She goes through her

act with Jonathan, telling him that he has no need for any woman because he has himself. He is lying on his back. As she sinks to her knees by him Nichols cuts between him and a shot of Louise several times. The camera is held on Louise so that the wall behind her looks as if it is going up. By cutting back and forth between Louise and Jonathan it looks as if Louise is constantly moving down. Jonathan is also sinking (drowning?) in his fantasy. The Indian music on the phonograph gets faster and faster.
She says:

[You are] a real man, a kind man. . . . I don't mean weak kind, the way so many men are. I mean the kindness that comes from enormous strength, from an inner power so strong that every act, no matter what, is more proof of that power. That's what all women resent. That's why they try to cut you down. Because your knowledge of yourself—and them—is so right, so true, that it exposes the lies which they, every scheming one of them, live by. It takes a true woman to understand that the purest form of love is to love a man who denies himself to her. A man who inspires worship because he has no need for any woman because he has himself. And who is better? More beautiful, more powerful, more perfect—you're getting hard—more strong, more masculine, extraordinary, more robust—it's rising, it's rising!—more virile, domineering, more irresistible! It's up . . . in the air!

Jonathan, smiling, is totally caught up in his fantasy now. He is complete in himself. The camera is on Jonathan's face. We hear the skating music, there is a fade to white, and we see the ice skater. She skates for a moment, and then fades out, and the screen goes to white. Closing credits roll over white. So the film ends with Jonathan in fantasy and with his ideal woman, the untouchable skater, ever present.

Carnal Knowledge is very well designed. For example, the film progresses through three time periods and Jonathan's inability to relate to a real woman is greater in each subsequent time period. The film begins in the forties, when Jonathan and Sandy are college students. This time period ends when Sandy and Susan go off on their honeymoon. The sixties is the period when Jonathan and Bobbie have their affair. It ends with Bobbie's attempted suicide. The seventies contain the slide show, "Ball Busters on Parade," Jonathan and Sandy talking for the last time, and the visit Jonathan pays to the prostitute.

Women begin each period. Jonathan and Sandy discuss women

during the credits, but the first person we see is Susan, alone, entering the college mixer. The transition from the forties to the sixties is done with the figure of the woman skater. The transition to the seventies is done with the slide show of the women in Jonathan's life. And the film ends with the image of the skater.

The temperature suggests the emotional climate in the relations between men and women. As Jonathan's relationships with women deteriorate, he becomes colder and more isolated. It is fall on the campus; dead leaves are blowing in the wind. Later, snow is seen on the ground. It is winter in New York when we first see the skater dressed in white, who is cold, untouchable, covered up, and skating through his life. This image also ends the film. Susan and Sandy will spend their honeymoon in the tropics, but Jonathan will remain in the cold.

The picture also moves from soft to hard in its overall look. Many symbolic elements are used to provide this "feel" in the film. One is color. Nichols' production designer, Richard Sylbert, who has worked on all of Nichols' films, explained it this way during the shooting:

> It's true there is little color, but it's not because of a conscious avoidance of color. It's a visual way of growing from college—which I always assumed was the color of a paper bag—to the 1970's. You see people differently in 1970 from the way they looked in 1946. There is a change in contrast. Back in college, under the tans and browns and brick colors, the edge was very soft. With time, life takes on a very hard edge. The mature man wearing a black velvet suit in a white room is, in every way, drastically different from the boy he was in college, with his khaki pants and khaki room and khaki bedspreads and khaki book covers. As the emotional pressures of the film's story increase, the contrast—which was soft and delicate in the beginning—will harden up. This is the effect that Peppino [cinematographer Giuseppe Rotunno, ASC] will be striving for, as shooting progresses.[1]

There is a simplicity in the visual symbols. Sylbert says: "We're trying to keep the picture very simple in the visual area. Since there are only four actors in it, other than extras, you might compare it to "chamber music." For this reason, we decided to stick to a few simple textures and simple colors."[2]

This is an appropriate design, for as the characters concentrate on one thing, their feelings about women, the style of the film complements this concentration.

The women wear primarily cold colors (white, black, or blue). And that's how Jonathan sees women, as people who are black and white, without shades of gray, or cold, as indicated by the blues. Nichols often has his women wear black to be played off against a white or yellowish background. He may owe a great debt to Antonioni, especially to Antonioni's film, *Red Desert*, where the outward colors reflect the inner states of the characters.

Like one of Feiffer's cartoons, the characters are not "filled in." We don't know very much about Jonathan and Sandy, except how they interact with each other and how they feel about women. Just like the characters, the backgrounds also tend not to be filled in. Sylbert speaks of walking into the set and subtracting things, reducing things to a bare minimum.[3] Since the sets and the characters are not filled in, it is up to the viewer to complete them. *Carnal Knowledge* demands the concentration of the viewer. Everything is not clearly laid out for him as in, say, an episode of a western on television.

Nichols also uses music that comes primarily from sources in the film, and he uses that music symbolically, relating it to the "spine" of the work.

Nichols' form and techniques are clear, but there are some underlying meanings and implications in the content. For example, the women do not fare well in *Carnal Knowledge*. Susan tells Sandy she wants to be a lawyer and write novels, but she becomes a housewife. She knowingly dates Jonathan and Sandy, but does not tell Sandy. From what little we know of her, she seems to have conflicting feelings about sex. She seems attracted to Sandy because of his sensitivity and his safeness. And she certainly has the dominant role in the relationship. While they are packing for the tropics, she calls Sandy "silly," a "real city boy," a "baby," and a "nut." With Jonathan she plays a subordinate role. In the scene when he makes love to her while wearing a fur coat, he looks like a bear on top of her. He is definitely on top, or dominant, in their relationship. This seems to frighten her. She doesn't seem to enjoy sex during the scene we see, but later it is learned that she and Jonathan do it "standing, sitting, in the car, under the car." She knows that both Jonathan and Sandy love her. She is attracted to Jonathan sexually, but she chooses to love the safer character. She might have fared better with Jonathan. They enjoyed sex together and he also said with conviction that he loved her. She may have been able also to accept the growing emotional feelings she had for Jonathan (she cries when they break up) and eventually may have been able to combine loving and sexual feelings. Susan is a tragic character. She does not realize her potential either in her sex life or in her career. Her marriage is also unfulfilled. And by choosing safe Sandy, Susan reaffirmed in Jonathan's mind that women were indeed ball busters and paved the way for Jonathan's recurring acts with other women.

Susan is never seen again live after the 1940s section of the film. She disappears when she loses her value principally as a sexual object. But her presence is felt, and she is included in Jonathan's "Ball Busters on Parade" slide show.

Bobbie is also a tragic character. She desperately wants to get married. But Jonathan does not want marriage. When Bobbie shacks up with him, she quits her job to please him. She significantly serves him food in bed. But Jonathan is interested in sexual satisfaction, and he tries not to allow the other aspects of the relationship to grow. Bobbie becomes more and more depressed about not being married (although, as their subsequent divorce indicates, this marriage did not change the quality of her relationship with Jonathan) and sleeps constantly. When she finally takes an overdose of pills, Jonathan sees it as her manipulating him into marrying her. By having marriage the one goal, Bobbie leads an incomplete and tragic life.

In regard to Cindy, Joan Mellen has this to say: " 'Maybe it's just not meant to be enjoyable with women you love,' says Sandy, with Nichols and Feiffer refusing to grant the truth of what they have dramatized—that the women whose only outlet for their emotional energy is the sexual soon lose both sexual desire and appeal, so shrunken do their sensibilities become. Only Cindy, the female counterpart to Jonathan, totally selfish and self-serving, escapes this dilemma. . . . Her sexual autonomy is maintained at the price of absolute bitchiness."[4]

And Cindy doesn't seem to have a fulfilling life with Sandy as their relationship is eventually terminated. And perhaps even the relationship that Jennifer, the love child, has with Sandy is a dead relationship. She exhibits little sexual appeal. Sandy says of her, in a complimentary way to Jonathan, "She's my love teacher." Note that it's not "sex teacher." It reminds me of Sandy's notion that he would rather be in love, trying to spiritualize relationships. Perhaps with

Sandy, as with other Nichols characters, there is not enough changed, and Sandy will continue to live out his fantasies about women through Jennifer and perhaps others later on.

In their relationships with these women, then, Jonathan and Sandy do not change their outlooks. Remember that they are both dressed in brown at the end of the film. Brown carries back to their "paper bag" college days. They have not changed in their relationship. Only their relationship together remains, while the women come and go.

The college background in the forties helps establish the rootlessness of the major characters. College has practically no effect on them. In fact, the characters have very little feeling about the colleges. Sandy feels he is being pressured into going to school. Sandy and Susan both hate college mixers for it is "such a phony way of meeting people." When asked by Susan how he likes Amherst, Sandy replies, "Sure, why shouldn't I? My parents worked hard to send me. I'd better like it." When asked about Smith College, Susan says unenthusiastically that she "likes it all right." The characters never speak of college life. When Susan is asked by Jonathan if she likes Smith, she asks, "What's your major?" He answers with, "Where did you go to high school?"

The campus itself is a dreary place. The room where the mixer is being held is dreary yellow, drab in contrast to the passionate red temporarily associated with sex. The yellow appears in the dorm room, which is sparsely furnished (more like a cell than a room) with beds that have bars on them. We never see the campus looking cheerful. The scenes are either at night or on the winter days with gray skies.

The distressing thing about the college in *Carnal Knowledge* is that it is so insignificant. It doesn't help prepare these people for the problems they will eventually face in life; it only teaches them to become doctors or tax lawyers—just as in *The Graduate* Benjamin must begin learning what's important after he leaves college. The real education takes place after graduation or somewhere else.

The college in this film might as well not exist. How can one cope with a college that is meaningless, a backdrop? And this is the problem that emerges from three of Nichols' films. The college is meaningless except to enable one to get a job in the world of plastics!

Jonathan and Sandy concentrate on women and sex. The viewer
must concentrate on what selected information is provided and read
back out of the images and sounds the meaning of the film.

Newsweek sees *Carnal Knowledge* as "the story of two young men
who grow older without growing up, who travel through time without changing, who live out destinies that are already drawn by the
lines of their limited selves."[5] In other words, Jonathan and Sandy
may change women, but their attitudes remain the same. So no
matter with whom they are, the drama continues, world without
end. They live out their fantasies with their women, no matter who
the women are or what they do.

Near the beginning of the film Susan tells Sandy, "I think people
only like to think they're putting on an act, but it's not an act, it's
really them. If they think it's an act they feel better because they
think they can always change it."

At the end of the film Louise, the prostitute, is putting on an act
for Jonathan in order to stimulate him sexually. In fact, when she
says a line differently than she has many times in the past, he
becomes very upset and corrects her. Sandy is also continuing to act
out his fantasies with his "love child" at the end of the film. The sad
thing about the characters in *Carnal Knowledge* is that they are
caught in an act, so to speak, that repeats itself endlessly, and an act
that is very real to them.

Even though Jonathan and Sandy's relationship is the only one
that continues through the film, I don't think Nichols is making a
case for homosexuality or is saying that sexual relationships between
two men are better than relationships between a man and a woman.
This would defeat the very point of the picture. Jonathan and
Sandy's relationship endures because it is not sexual; neither man is
capable of handling a physical relationship with another person.
Sandy and Jonathan cannot relate lovingly and sexually to women,
but they don't relate lovingly and sexually to each other, either.
Sandy and Jonathan both want to get laid by women, not each other.
They help each other remain perpetually college boys. Nichols
seems concerned with how perceptions determine relationships.

Near the beginning of the film, Sandy says, "I feel the same way
about getting laid as I feel about going to college. I'm getting pressured into it."

When asked about this line, Feiffer replied, "It's a result of the
society that the Jonathans and Sandys were born into, the mythol-

ogy they were reared in from birth, which geared them to think about themselves as men and about their relationship with women. They were trained to think about women as conveniences, receptacles, appendages . . . it had to do with rivalry and envy, with competition with the other fellows, more than it had to do with women."[6]

In a sequence later cut from the film, perhaps because it made the theme too explicit, Jonathan says to a young woman, "Remember when you were a kid and the boys didn't like the girls? Only sissies liked girls? What I am trying to tell you is that nothing has changed. You think boys grow out of not liking girls, but we don't grow out of it. We just grow horny. That's the problem. We mix up liking pussy with liking girls. Believe me, one couldn't have less to do with the other."[7]

Stefan Kanfer of *Time* says in his review that the subtext of the film carries the chill of fastidious puritanism: Sex is dirty; touch it and you get a disease.[8] I don't think, however, the characters are punished because they have sex. The film is not an old-fashioned melodrama in which the characters are punished because they indulge in extramarital sex. In *Carnal Knowledge* the characters are hurt not because they have sex, but because of their narrow, selfish preconceptions about sex and women which determine that their relationships will be incomplete.

In his brilliant *The Denial of Death*, Ernest Becker sees *Carnal Knowledge* as a contrast between the romantic (Sandy) and the sensualist (Jonathan): "Both of these types meet, in the film, on the middle ground of utter confusion about what one should get out of a world of breasts and buttocks and of rebellion against what the species demands of them. The sensualist tries to avoid marriage with all his might, to defeat the species role by making sexuality a purely personal affair of conquests and virility. The romantic rises above marriage and sex by trying to spiritualize his relationship to women. Neither type can understand the other except on the level of elemental physical desire; and the film leaves us with the reflection that both are pitifully immersed in the blind groping of the human condition, the reaching out for an absolute that can be seen and experienced."[9]

Nichols has exaggerated and polarized the two extremes: Jonathan's, where a woman is only a sex object, and Sandy's, where a woman is only someone to love. As Sandy says, "Maybe it's [sex is] just not meant to be enjoyable with women you love." Sex and love cannot meet in these two polarized extremes. Relationships must remain incomplete. The characters see love and sex as separate. That is the tragedy. Nichols shows us that these extreme preconceptions ruin the characters' lives. (Recall that in *The Graduate* Mrs. Robinson was presented as sensual and Elaine as romantic.) By showing us that these preconceptions are what is causing the characters so much unhappiness, Nichols is forcing us to examine our own preconceptions.

Certainly *Carnal Knowledge* shares with the other Nichols works similar characteristics. In "Pictures of Innocence," in *Sight and Sound*, in which John Lindsay Brown describes Nichols as an *auteur* film director, he sees Nichols, in *Who's Afraid of Virginia Woolf?*, *The Graduate*, and *Carnal Knowledge*, as exploring the sexual strata of relationships in middle-class America. This society is self-made and reasonably well off, oriented toward education in terms of status, vaguely liberal, and morally sophisticated. "The view of these relationships which all three films present is a pessimistic one, with exploitation and self-destructiveness the recurring characteristics. Moreover, Nichols habitually charts the same line of dramatic tension through his material, a line which can be summed up as the varieties of defeat suffered by innocence in its confrontations with experience."[10] This latter insight is a brilliant one indeed, and it applies to all six of Nichols' films, although we shall explore later the question of whether innocence is *really* defeated in Nichols' films.

Brown also points out that the characters in *Carnal Knowledge* have their origins in earlier Nichols films. Sandy is a version of Benjamin in *The Graduate*, Jonathan resembles the selfish, aggressive Nick from *Who's Afraid of Virginia Woolf?* Susan is reminiscent of Elaine (although I feel she is more like a younger Mrs. Robinson), and Cindy is reminiscent of Mrs. Robinson and Martha. (A detailed look at this whole argument is rewarding.) However, Brown's insights about the characters are useful to our analysis. Sandy, Benjamin, Jonathan, and Nick have destructive relationships with certain women. In *The Graduate* and *Who's Afraid of Virginia Woolf?* there is a destructive relationship between an older woman and a younger man.

Many of the characters are manipulators. For example, Jonathan is a manipulator. He cynically manipulates women and watches his effect on them. He is very selfish. When he learns that Susan has masturbated Sandy on a date, he manipulates her into a date with him and eventually beds her. We can see his manipulatory technique from this passage: "Hello, is this Susan? Well, you don't know me. I'm a friend of Sandy's, his roommate. Yeah, Jonathan. He told you about me? Yeah, so I'm just here at Smith for tonight, practically on campus. I was taking a drive, you know, and I found myself practically on campus. . . ."

When Susan asks, "Do you always date your best friend's girl?" Jonathan replies, "Sandy told me you were beautiful."

Susan is also a manipulator. She has an affair with two men at once. She dominates Sandy, which can be seen clearly in the scene when they prepare to go to the tropics. She calls him "a city boy," "a nut," "a baby." She obviously has the upper hand. She is somewhat like Martha in *Who's Afraid of Virginia Woolf?* In describing the character of Martha, another manipulator, as he envisioned it, Nichols has said, "The brilliant, over-educated, ball-cutting woman who has womanly feelings and alternates between them is a very specific type. . . . It's that very specific poet's wife, or professor's wife, whose hair escapes from the knot at the back of her head, whose dream doesn't quite fit, who's read everything, and laughs at Simone de Beauvoir, and who says, what in effect Martha said in the play: 'Abstruse in the sense of recondite. Don't you tell me words.' "[11] This description is very close to Susan.

Jonathan sees Bobbie as a manipulator, even though she does not display manipulative characteristics. She just wants to get married, have children, and make Jonathan the center of her life. Jonathan sums it up, "My wife, the fastest tits in the West, but king of the ball-busters. She conned me into marrying her, and now she's killing me with alimony." Jonathan sees Bobbie as an object, a pair of tits. She is called a ball-buster (which, in reality, she is not) and a con artist.

Louise, the prostitute, manipulates men for money. She has figured out Jonathan perfectly and plays upon his selfish attitudes toward women.

Another characteristic that *Carnal Knowledge* shares with the other Nichols films is many, long continuous takes in which the characters talk to each other. Good examples of this device can be found in the scenes where Sandy talks to Jonathan about his marriage with Susan and the first scene of the film while the characters talk over the credits.

The motif of water runs symbolically through the film. Jonathan jumps in the pool to tell Sandy he is no longer a virgin. He is continually taking showers. The showers are almost a ritualistic cleaning up after becoming "dirty" by sex or talking about sex (so that there is some residual puritanism contaminating the characters' two-dimensional sexual attitudes). The showers also prevent communication between Jonathan and Bobbie. And there is the frozen water that the woman skates on. Like the frozen water, Jonathan is cold and dead in his affectionate feelings toward women.

Nichols' major male figure searching for something is Jonathan, although Sandy is also searching. They are searching for a meaningful sexual and loving relationship with a woman. Destructive women interact with the male figure. Especially destructive are Susan, Cindy, and Louise. Bobbie is also destructive, although she does not mean to be.

The environment too becomes more sterile and hostile throughout the film. The walls lose their color, the images become harder and more barren.

There is a turning point in the film when the main male character makes a decision. This is purposely near the beginning at the end of the 1940s sequence, when Jonathan and Susan talk on the phone. Susan chooses Sandy over Jonathan, and her rejection is clear from this conversation. Jonathan earlier told her that he loved her. He said earlier in the film to Sandy that he wouldn't want to get hurt. "Every time I start being in love, the girl does something that turns me cold," he says. Susan, by rejecting Jonathan, has hurt him irrevocably. When the ice skater is seen shortly after Susan's rejection, we assume that Jonathan has symbolically "turned cold" in his affectionate feelings toward women.

Jonathan has made a decision. It is a decision based only partly on the fact that no matter what he does Susan will probably go with Sandy. Jonathan decides not to fight Sandy for her or to tell Sandy about his relationship with her. He chooses instead not to harm his relationship with Sandy. He, in effect, decides in favor of Sandy's friendship and against anything but sexual relationships with women in the future. He now checks with Sandy before trying to bed Cindy. The key line comes as Sandy and Jonathan are walking in the 1970s. Jonathan says, "Sandy, I love you but you're a schmuck." Jonathan loves Sandy, and that love becomes more important than love with Susan or any woman. It is not physical love. If Susan had chosen Jonathan, there might have been a slim hope for a loving sexual relationship. But that would have been another movie, not a Nichols film.

Although as in the other films religion is ridiculed here (in the tavern where Jonathan, Susan, and Sandy make fun of the words of hymns), religion does not seem to be a major force in the characters' lives in this film.

The idea that sex and love are separated, with sex destructive and love constructive, certainly does appear in this film. In fact, it is almost the basis for it. Sandy says, "Maybe it's just not meant to be enjoyable with women you love."

And finally, there is the sad, pessimistic ending. The main male character, Jonathan, is lost forever in his fantasies and preconceptions. The other male character, Sandy, may have gained understanding with Jennifer, but we doubt it. He still has his fantasies about women. He certainly has not gained true freedom. The final irony of the title is that "carnal knowledge" is just that and nothing more—a knowledge of other people as just "meat"—mindless things to be manipulated. Carnal knowledge doesn't guarantee that one possesses knowledge of any other kind.

Nichols' style is moving from the real to the abstract. *Who's Afraid of Virginia Woolf?* was firmly anchored in reality. Objects filled the frame. The focus was sharp. *The Graduate* was also based in reality, but the manipulation of cinematic devices was much more in evidence; the clever cutting, the varied sounds, the many symbols. *Catch-22* moved further from realism and took place in one character's mind. Time was altered. Images and sounds became more abstract. Yossarian's face floated into frame. Scenes were overexposed and done in slow motion. With *Carnal Knowledge* images are simplified even further. Only essential objects are included in the frame. Heads float in and out. The background is blurred on many occasions—when Susan is laughing in close-up, and when Jonathan and Sandy are walking along the street in New York. *Carnal Knowledge* is a beautiful film to watch with the soundtrack turned off because of the visual design elements. Nichols composes for the wide screen, and his images are indeed simplified and beautiful.

Stanley Kauffman writes of *Carnal Knowledge*, "Nichols is concentrating more and more on the frame—the held shot—as a source of power. . . . It's a use of the camera as watcher, as *drainer*, rather than as participant—surely not the only way to use the camera but one that implies a growing stillness in the director, a sense of security, of serious fundamental decisions."[12]

Carnal Knowledge has important things to say about contemporary sexual mores and values, relationships between men and women, and how one's view of an event shapes that event.

The film represents a further development of themes that were taboo on the American screen. As with *Who's Afraid of Virginia Woolf?*, *The Graduate*, and somewhat with *Catch-22*, Nichols is dealing with subjects that often have been thought of as too daring for the screen. And he handles these subjects artistically and with great integrity. Censorship problems were also in evidence with the release of *Carnal Knowledge*.[13] Beginning with *Who's Afraid of Virginia Woolf?* Nichols has blazed a trail for himself and for others to follow in dealing with mature and important subjects on film.

6

The Day of the Dolphin

AFTER FILMING *Carnal Knowledge,* Nichols returned to Broadway and directed Neil Simon's play, *The Prisoner of Second Avenue,* in the fall of 1971. He won a Tony award for best director. Then, in 1973, he directed Anton Chekhov's *Uncle Vanya,* in a new translation by Nichols and Albert Todd, at the Circle in the Square Theatre. In the cast was George C. Scott, whom he would use in his fifth film, *The Day of the Dolphin,* in 1973.

The Day of the Dolphin is based on the book of the same title by Robert Merle, published in 1967. The script was written by Buck Henry, who also wrote the scripts for *The Graduate* and *Catch-22.*

The story is about Dr. Jake Terrell, a marine biologist, who in his island laboratory is trying to teach dolphins to speak English. The project is funded by the Franklin Foundation. Unknown to Terrell, Harold DeMilo, who is with the Foundation, is plotting with a group of men to assassinate the President of the United States. Terrell is successful with his experiments and teaches two dolphins, Alpha and Beta, to speak. The dolphins are then kidnapped by DeMilo's men who plan to use them to blow up the presidential yacht. Alpha escapes and the assassination attempt is foiled. Terrell tells the dolphins to return to the sea and speak to no one again. He and his wife are on the island when members of the assassination group come to the island to destroy all evidence and presumably kill them because of their knowledge of the assassination plot.

To analyze *The Day of the Dolphin* I find Constance Rourke's method useful; she uses myth—that is, any suggestive fable or legend—to analyze formal art in relation to its roots in folk tradition.[1]

The idea of a dedicated doctor teaching dolphins to speak English is reminiscent of several myths: Prometheus bringing fire to man (and being punished for it); Jesus Christ spreading the word to man

The Day of the Dolphin.
Courtesy of the Museum of Modern Art/Film Stills Archive.

(and being punished for it); Frankenstein creating a man (and being punished for it); and countless other tales that use this idea of the benevolent benefactor coming to grief. In keeping with this theme, *The Day of the Dolphin* is really not so much about what happens to the dolphins as about what happens to Dr. Jake Terrell himself. He is the man spreading the word, so to speak. And he is indeed punished for it. Other traditions are also to be found here: the idea of the pastoral, simple island where Dr. Terrell and his dolphins can communicate apart from the rest of the world; the theme of the destruction of the private paradise, which can be found from *Peter Pan* (with Captain Hook) to *Billy Jack* (with Bernard Posner); and themes of loss of innocence (both the dolphins' and Terrell's) and of man's rape of nature.

So, because of all these mythical implications one should not dismiss this picture lightly, although some critics did; perhaps they just could not accept the idea of talking dolphins. Some people may also have rejected the film because they found parts of it were so painful. Part of the pain may stem from the several levels of manipulation that are going on. I pointed out in previous chapters that many of Nichols' characters are manipulators. In this film we see manipulation on a grand and sometimes hurtful scale. The dolphins are manipulated by Terrell. Terrell is manipulated by the Franklin Foundation. And we, the viewers, are in turn manipulated by Nichols.

Dr. Terrell is fascinated by the dolphins. He says that they are instinct and energy and that we should become like them. He wears cool gray at the beginning of the film, his outer skin of clothing the same color as a dolphin. In the first scene of the film, he describes the wonders of the dolphins, and we see the dolphins intercut with tight shots of him talking. This intercutting between the dolphins and Terrell connects them in the viewer's mind.

Terrell teaches the dolphins to speak, to be like him, to be almost human. They have experience with some men, who as Terrell tells them, are "bad." But Terrell is basically a good man. And he has not only taught the dolphins language, but some of his goodness, man's goodness. It is because of Terrell that Alpha knows right from wrong, escapes the "bad" men, and foils the plot to kill the President. The ending of the film is indeed ironic. Alpha and Beta go back to the sea (by orders of Terrell) and will speak to no one. But they carry with them man's symbolic structures of right and wrong, good and evil, hate and love. They are no longer instinct and energy, and they have lost their innocence through their relationship with a man. Their experiences have important mythic implications.

In the first shot of the film, we see a dolphin close up and then some credits, including the title, are superimposed over him. The dolphin's eye is looking directly at us. The next shot is of Terrell, his suit the color of the dolphin's skin; he too is looking at us and giving a lecture on dolphins. There follow cuts between what Terrell is saying and images of the dolphin. We see a dolphin leap into the air with a ball in his mouth in slow motion. He already is carrying something created by man. There is beautiful music on the sound track. We see the dolphin being trained to recognize different shapes. A man shows the dolphin pictures of shapes on cards, and then the dolphin swims out and retrieves floating objects in those shapes. When shown a shape that is no longer in the sea, the dolphin recognizes the trick. He is not fooled.

Curtis Mahoney, who seems at first to be an enemy of Terrell, but later turns out to be a friend who is spying on the Foundation, is seen in these shots watching the man and the dolphin. Terrell, in close-up, discusses the speech sounds (clicks) that a dolphin makes. We then see a dolphin with wires attached to its skull. Terrell denounces this kind of experiment as cruel. He is not just addressing the viewer; he is lecturing to an audience within the film. He now shows a film of Alpha's birth to that audience and to us. Then the lights go on and we see the people in the auditorium clearly. This very clever way of getting into the picture is almost the reverse of the film's major design, which moves from the complex to the simple, from civilization to Terrell's island, to Terrell himself, and finally to the dolphin. The opening reverses this order by showing the dolphin, then only Terrell, then Terrell on stage, and then the members of the audience. Terrell answers questions from the audience. He says he doesn't know about military experiments with dolphins. He wonders why dolphins, who are mammals, returned to the sea. He says that the dolphin someone saw counting in English is a trick. Mahoney is in the audience and there is sinister music on the soundtrack.

We are introduced to Harold DeMilo, executive of the Franklin Foundation, who poses as a friend of Terrell, but who will later betray him as part of the plot to take the dolphins and kill the

President. He may be a reincarnation of another Milo from *Catch-22*, the great manipulator for money and power. In brilliant parallel construction, DeMilo looks like a friend but is really an enemy, while Mahoney looks like an enemy but is really a friend.

The scene with DeMilo functions in three ways. One, it introduces DeMilo and establishes him as the one who oversees the foundation money for Terrell. Two, it sets up a conflict between the two characters about this money, and the tension is increased by the ominous music and acting style. Three, it establishes that Terrell will do things for DeMilo in order to keep the Foundation happy. It is for DeMilo that Terrell is giving the speech when he would rather be on the island with the dolphins. This scene sets up a much later scene when Terrell goes to a phony press conference for DeMilo. That he suddenly leaves for this conference is made believable, for the viewer has already seen Terrell come to land for DeMilo.

In the opening scenes, then, the parallel between Terrell and the dolphins is reinforced. Terrell comes to land from his island and feels uncomfortable giving a speech (as the dolphins, Terrell indicates later, feel uncomfortable in their speech). All Terrell wants to do is get back to the island as fast as possible. On the mainland he feels as uncomfortable and helpless as a fish on land. Like Alpha, who when out of water is at man's mercy, he is at DeMilo's mercy when out of his environment. To show his anger at DeMilo, Terrell has DeMilo drive him from the lecture to the marina, which is a considerable distance away.

On the boat at the marina, it is learned that Maggie, Terrell's wife, has been injured by Alpha. The boat driver from the island tells Terrell that Maggie is tough. Terrell says that he is worried about Alpha. Here the idea is introduced that Terrell may prefer dolphins to people.

The boat leaves the marina in the daytime and approaches the island in the evening, indicating that the island is a fairly long distance from the mainland, where the lecture took place and where the marina is. On the island are several buildings which serve as laboratories and living quarters. Terrell is upset that Alpha was left alone in his tank when his assistant took Maggie to the house. Terrell is told that Alpha bit Maggie on the leg when she was in the tank because he was sexually excited by her. Terrell says, "I go away for one lousy afternoon—the whole place falls apart." This is an important line, for it establishes how important Terrell feels he is to those around him (he is in complete control), and also prepares the viewer for the next time Terrell leaves (for the phony press conference), when things really fall apart. To this Maggie replies, "Getting jealous?" This is a nice reversal, for it is Maggie who should be jealous about the time Terrell spends with Alpha. In fact, she tells him to go to Alpha as she knows about his concern for the dolphin.

It takes a long time to go through the tank room and to the tank. I feel this is part of the design of the film; it suggests that Terrell is leaving the complex (civilization) and entering the simple (dolphin in tank). In leaving Maggie, Terrell must travel a distance and through things before reaching Alpha (just as the boat traveled a long distance from land to the island).

The dolphin comes up and calls "Pa," the name he uses for Terrell. Terrell calls him "Fa." He explained earlier that "Fa" is simplified from "Alpha," but since the two words sound so alike, it is another instance of equating the man and the dolphin. Terrell pets him. The next shot is of Maggie alone in the house. She has trouble walking. The camera moves outside, and the island and its buildings are revealed in a long panning shot. There is a dissolve into the tank and then the camera moves into the window and the water. We see Terrell and Alpha swimming together. Beautiful music is heard on the soundtrack. Terrell pets Alpha, turns him over, touches him, even rides him. We see the wedding band on Terrell's hand.

In this entire scene from Maggie alone to Terrell and Alpha swimming together, Nichols has employed visual effects brilliantly to articulate several meanings. Maggie limps awkwardly while her husband and the dolphin swim gracefully and happily. This is especially significant when we remember that the dolphin caused Maggie's limp. Terrell prefers to swim with Alpha rather than to be with Maggie. Even the wedding band shown on Terrell's hand as he touches the dolphin visually states that Terrell is finding not physical love, of course, but happiness and companionship and loving feelings with the dolphin. They swim/dance together as in a ballet, a work of art. Terrell's love and attachment for Alpha is clear, and also implicit in the action is the notion that he would like to be a dolphin. To him, humans are imperfect. Dolphins, as he says later, are "instinct and energy." Alpha and Terrell swim as one; they are happy; air bubbles rise to the surface.

There is a dissolve to the ocean. DeMilo's head enters the frame. The ocean outside DeMilo's office is seen through the window, and we are now in his office. This is a fine transition. Nichols goes from water in the tank to water in the ocean, using water as a connecting link. DeMilo's head is then seen large, and this is a visual symbol. DeMilo is the one who will interrupt Terrell's world. He will loom large over Terrell and his world as his head looms large in the frame. And, of course, it is very appropriate to show the complete happiness of Terrell and Alpha right before DeMilo raises his head over the water.

Mahoney, the man who is watching the Foundation, is in DeMilo's office. He tells DeMilo that he wants to write an article on Terrell and the island. When DeMilo refuses, he threatens to write an article about the Foundation and DeMilo's past. (We learn later of the Foundation's shady doings and DeMilo's homosexuality.) DeMilo decides to let Mahoney visit the island.

Back at the island, DeMilo interrupts the work there when he arrives in a seaplane. He says, "Beautiful, simply beautiful. It's like being in another world." This remark emphasizes the pastoral and isolated setting. DeMilo, Terrell, and Maggie sit and talk. When Terrell learns that the Board of Directors of the Foundation are thinking of withdrawing their support, Terrell and DeMilo walk to the lab. Terrell wishes to show DeMilo what he is doing so support won't be cut off. Inside the lab, Terrell plays tapes of Alpha's voice at various stages in his learning to speak. There are rows and rows of tape recorders, and he lets one continue to play as he starts the next one, until they are all playing. Alpha says only words, not sentences.

We see shots of DeMilo, who is impressed, and of Alpha. In a water transition Alpha swims out of view and there is a cut to more water where a wild female dolphin is swimming. Terrell will give Alpha a female partly to make him happier and encourage him to speak faster and partly, perhaps, to stop his sexual advances toward Maggie. DeMilo indicates that he will keep what he has seen confidential and that the funds should continue; but he asks Terrell to do him the favor of letting Mahoney visit the island. Terrell agrees, and we see the two men talking from where Maggie is standing a long distance away on the porch. Nichols is showing us her uneasiness at what is going on.

Alpha and the female dolphin, whom Terrell names Beta, swim together. They don't talk when Terrell tries to give them fish. Terrell thinks that Alpha is learning his own dolphin language from Beta. Maggie says, while watching the dolphins, "It's love all right."

In the next scene, Mahoney is on the boat that will bring him to the island. The fellow driving the boat avoids answering his questions. The boat tosses and turns, and Mahoney is definitely not enjoying himself.

On the island, Terrell prepares to separate the two dolphins in order to force Alpha to speak. But Mahoney arrives on the island just as Terrell is about to make the separation. This timing may suggest that Mahoney can be seen as a threat who will tell the world about the talking dolphins and perhaps even separate Terrell and Alpha. Terrell plans to hide Alpha and Beta in a holding tank, but Alpha takes a wrench from Terrell and plays with him, keeping the wrench from him. Here is suggested a nice parallel to Mahoney, who will throw a "monkey wrench" into the works.

Mahoney gets out of the boat, and workers at the island put Alpha and Beta in the holding tank. When Mahoney asks to see Alpha, the workers, to cover up that Terrell is teaching Alpha to speak (so there will be no publicity), show him a different dolphin, for Terrell has many on the island.

Terrell and Maggie talk alone on the porch. Terrell realizes that Maggie doesn't trust Mahoney and the "good old establishment." He advises her to "leave it alone." This scene emphasizes the idea that Terrell is interested in his scientific work, not in the motivations behind the Foundation or the government. Terrell's awakening to his responsibility to be aware of political intrigues and his loss of innocence in this regard are major parts of the book on which the film is based. In the film, this matter is simplified, partly because in translating a novel to the screen characters and plots must be simplified. Also, as I shall suggest later, the book contains very powerful political intrigues which the filmmakers may not have wanted to deal with.

Mahoney becomes suspicious about which dolphin is the real Alpah when he is shown a dolphin he is told is Alpha which has a disfigured fin. One of the workers tells him that the fin was disfigured by a shark. Mahoney knows that Alpha was born in captivity. Another worker is quick to point out that the fin was disfigured on the island before the first worker arrived.

The next scene is inside the fish tank control room at night. A girl worker is frightened by a door handle moving, complete with scary music on the soundtrack. She calls Maggie, who gets up and looks out over the island buildings, but sees nothing important. In the morning Mahoney gives Terrell his phone number, says that they are all on the same side, and leaves.

Terrell now separates Alpha and Beta. Alpha, who still won't talk, bangs his tail on Beta's tank for hours. Nichols compresses these hours in filmic time by cutting from the tank to a girl sitting on the beach, to Maggie sleeping at night, and the like. Terrell is asleep at the side of the tank when Alpha speaks sentences as "Fa want Bi now." Terrell calls "Maggie" repeatedly and lights go on (as the light of knowledge turns on). Terrell opens the tank to let the dolphins be together, and both Alpha and Beta swim to classical-type music. This sequence ends with a shot of the workers bringing Terrell a cake to celebrate Alpha speaking in sentences. The cake is in the shape of a dolphin with a candle on it (more light, or wisdom, in the dark). Right at the end of this shot, Terrell turns to blow the candle out, a brilliant foreshadowing of the ending when he will tell Alpha and Beta to go to sea.

Terrell and a worker are on the pier, discussing what would happen if a shark got in Alpha and Beta's tank—nice symbolism for the "shark" DeMilo and his men. Terrell says they could call for help. He says he feels something he has not felt since he was young, that "there are infinite possibilities." However, only one candle has been lit in the dark.

The sharks do call, in the guise of the Foundation, to say that Mahoney has found out about the talking dolphins and will publish the story. Terrell, worried that the publicity and the exploitation that would go with it may interfere with his scientific work before it is completed, says, "They're sneaking up on us"; and the next shot is of Mahoney and a friend sneaking onto the island by boat.

What takes place now is a very important dialogue between Terrell and Maggie. They are both inside their home. He is worried about the world closing in. Maggie says that civilization will interfere with his little kingdom. Terrell says he is afraid of the diseases of the outside world that can kill Alpha and Beta, by turning them into valuable property. Now Terrell thinks about who is responsible. Maggie suggests that he is teaching the dolphins to talk to become like him. Terrell says that we should become like them, "instinct and energy." It becomes clearer here that Terrell would like to become like the dolphins, that he is upset with the world of man, and that he would indeed like to be "instinct and energy." Ironically, this is the side of Terrell which has gotten him into trouble. He is energy in his "tunnel vision" work with the dolphins and does things out of instinct, not thinking of the consequences or of the political and power struggles about him. He begins to question the good of what he has done and to think of possible harmful effects on Alpha and Beta. When Maggie suggests that he let them go, Terrell replies that it is too late, that he and Maggie have changed them, and that they wouldn't know what to do or where to go. Terrell doesn't seem to realize that there may be both positive and negative effects to the change.

Mahoney and his friend, hiding on the island, see the seaplane that has arrived bringing members of the Foundation to the island. Terrell has decided to make public his work with the dolphins in order, I feel, to present it scientifically and to control exploitation before Mahoney can publish his article. He will show the Foundation members first.

The dolphins answer questions posed by the Foundation members. Alpha—through his association with Terrell, Maggie, and the workers—feels that "man is good." Terrell says that dolphins don't know hypothetical terms yet, and that good to Alpha means, as Alpha says, smooth (a man's skin feels good to the touch, is smooth, and smooth is pleasure and pleasure is good). The viewer may be left with the impression that Alpha believes man is good in other ways. When asked later why he speakes when it is so difficult for him to do so, Alpha says that he loves Pa and indicates that he does it for Terrell because he loves him.

One of the Foundation men, discussing the dolphin's enemy, the shark, lies to Alpha and Beta, telling them that there is a shark in the tank. They have not been lied to before, so Beta quickly jumps out of the tank and into the ocean. Terrell calls to Alpha to bring Beta back; Alpha does so. This shows that he can bring her back, important later in the film, when he must stop her from placing a mine on the President's yacht. The notion of the innocent dolphins being lied to relates to the innocent Terrell who also has been lied to by DeMilo. So the dolphins and Terrell both lose their innocence in their parallel stories.

Mahoney and his friend, hidden in the foliage, watch the press conference end. DeMilo lies to Terrell to get him off the island so the assassination scheme can move forward; he tells him there is a press conference on land that he must attend. Since Maggie wants to go with him, they agree to leave.

On the boat Terrell asks why Mahoney was allowed to visit the island in the first place. DeMilo tells Terrell that Mahoney has a lot of influence with the government and has put pressure on the Foundation in order to visit the island. Terrell tells Maggie later that he will tell the world not only about the dolphins, but about Mahoney and the Foundation seeming to want to cover something up.

Mahoney's friend goes to look around the island. He is in the control room with a flashlight when he is suddenly hit on the head. Later that night, there is a phone call to the island, and one of the workers, David, takes it. He says it is from Terrell who has ordered the workers to place the dolphins on a boat that is located ominously offshore.

In the Franklin Foundation, with its cold white walls and windows looking out on the sea, Terrell is separated from his ocean physically. Mrs. Rome, an executive secretary to Foundation Director Simon, says that Mr. Simon has been taken ill, has been rushed to the hospital, and that DeMilo is with him. She says that there will be no press conference and that "we'll just have to tread water" (an appropriate metaphor). Icy Mrs. Rome is appropriately dressed in white.

Terrell calls the island from a pay phone and can't get through. He and Maggie return to the island and learn that Alpha and Beta have been kidnapped and that David lied to the other workers about receiving a call from Terrell. He also lied to the dolphins, it is learned later, when he had the workers tell them that Terrell was on the boat.

It is night and raining (the environment commenting on the mood of the characters) when Mahoney arrives, motioning for all to be quiet. He finds a wire tap and, after all go outside, explains that David is not the real name of the worker. David was trained in demolition when in the navy. When David was sentenced to a long prison term for smuggling heroin across the border, the Foundation got him released in eight months, and he now works for the Foundation.

Mahoney explains that he knows this because people pay him to watch the Foundation. Other people are watching him, he conjectures, just as Terrell and Maggie are watching the dolphins. He says that one might call the Foundation and its respectable businessmen part of the government and indicates that he also may be part of the government. He explains that there are many parts of the government, and that two or three million people work for it, not including the military. This theme seems to be handled in a cautious, roundabout way by Henry and Nichols. They suggest ideas to the viewers but do not come right out and say anything about alleged government connections. Mahoney also tells how he forced DeMilo to let him come to the island by threatening to publish information about the Foundation and DeMilo's homosexuality.

DeMilo calls and tells Terrell not to try to interfere or leave the island. Terrell and the group later find that the records and tapes of their experiments with Alpha and Beta have been taken or destroyed. They also find Mahoney's friend has been killed. When the light is switched on, there is a scream and then a zoom in to the dead man floating upside down underwater by the tank window with a chain around his neck fastened to a weight on the bottom. Here is an attempt by Nichols not only to shock the viewer, but to indicate visually that something very sinister is going on. This also illustrates the ruthlessness of the villains and the dangerous spot Terrell, his friends, and his dolphins are in. As Mahoney says later, "If they kill a man, what will stop them from killing dolphins?"

The next scene is on the boat containing Alpha and Beta. We see David talking with the dolphins who are quite helpless. There is a cut to Terrell and his friends in the control room. They, too, are quite helpless.

At the boat, we see David test a mine that can be attached to a dolphin's back. When the dolphin swims under the boat, the mine will attach itself to the boat. We see the dolphins, the members of the Foundation (who were at the island), and DeMilo. On the island, Terrell realizes that the dolphins will be killed because they can talk. "He's [Alpha's] a witness."

On the boat with the dolphins, David shows them a flag that bears the insignia of the President of the United States. Alpha puts a dummy mine under a dummy boat which bears the President's flag. Now we can see why Nichols used the shots of the dolphins looking at shapes and retrieving objects at the beginning of the film. It was to prepare the viewer for this scene in which the dolphin places the mine under the boat. The earlier scene has already planted in the viewer's mind the fact that dolphins can perform this task. Thinking that this method of assassinating the President will succeed, DeMilo leaves in a seaplane.

Alpha swims to the boat and says he wants Pa. A Texan-type member of the Foundation (and the one who lied about the shark) says, "Pa's here," lying to Alpha again. Beta is on board, and it sounds as if the two dolphins are talking in their own language. The Texan gets a gun. Back on the island, Terrell and the others are letting the dolphins go. Sad music on the soundtrack reflects their feelings.

At the boat, Alpha won't cooperate, so the men start shooting at him in the water. He swims away. The men think they have probably killed him, but they plan to return to Terrell's and kill him if he has escaped. The boat leaves.

On the island, Mahoney has figured out that the men plan to use the dolphins to kill the President. Alpha returns and jumps into his pen in slow motion. This slow-motion effect accentuates the beauty and joyful feelings at his return. At the same time, on the boat, David is fixing the mine.

Nichols has been cutting between two parallel story lines: Terrell and David. In this way, he can move the action along quickly and show what is happening simultaneously at two different locations. He is also able to condense much action into a short time. For example, the next shot is of Terrell's boat following Alpha, trying to catch David's boat. Nichols did not have to show Terrell getting into his boat. He cut directly from the previous scene of David's boat to Terrell's boat. The viewer will accept that while the camera was on David's boat, Terrell was busy getting into his boat, even though the viewer did not see this.

On Terrell's boat, Mahoney throws his dead friend overboard to lighten the load. Why they were carrying the dead man in the first place is not clear. Perhaps it was for evidence. Perhaps it is to reveal more of Mahoney's character. He has no loyalty except to himself, and this helps explain his actions at the conclusion of the film.

Realizing that they cannot catch David's boat, Terrell calls to Alpha and tells him that the ball on Beta's back is not good, that it kills and will hurt man, and that he should bring Beta back. Terrell and his party will return to the island, as they have just enough gas to get back. When asked what they can do now, Terrell says, "There is nothing we can do. We are finished." In this last sentence Terrell is not merely stating that they can't catch the boat. He has just realized that all that he has tried to accomplish is indeed finished.

A cut to David's boat shows David saying to Beta that if she wants Fa, she first must put the ball on the boat. Beta leaves to do that.

Alpha arrives at David's boat, and then swims away in the direction that Beta took. Now there is a chase scene with many shots, quick cuts, and exciting music as Alpha searches for Beta. He finds her near the President's boat. They talk dolphin and turn around.

They put the mine on David's boat. There is a tilt up from the water to an area where the viewer can see into the boat. There is a click. David looks and we (and he) see the dolphins swim away. He says, "Oh shit," and the boat explodes.

The next scene is remarkable in that it is one continuous take with no cuts. The camera follows Mrs. Rome at the Foundation walking to DeMilo in his office. It leads her down the hall and then moves with her as she goes into his office. DeMilo places a report that she gives him (no doubt about the events that have just taken place) into a paper shredder. The smooth continuous action of the camera is a contrast from the sharp cuts of the chase and final explosion. This change in rhythm calms the viewer down and also shows in expository action that the mission is finished. There is a fine, motivated cut from the paper shredder to papers burning in a trash can as Terrell destroys what is left of his notes and material.

The dolphins return and Terrell and the others learn from them what happened. Alpha is even sad when he tells them that David "is not," meaning "no longer exists." Mahoney says that other men will come for the dolphins and that they have to get out of there. True to character, he leaves a few minutes later. Alpha says he loves Pa. Terrell says he knows. Alpha wants to stay with Terrell. Terrell tries to explain to Alpha that he and Beta must go away to the sea and not talk to man. He explains that some men who are not good will come and hurt Pa if they stay. If they go, they won't hurt Pa. (He is thinking of the dolphins' safety here.) Alpha thinks that Terrell may not love him, but they are assured that Terrell and Maggie do indeed love Beta and him. A seaplane is approaching, no doubt carrying Foundation men who will kill all to cover up the assassination attempt. Terrell tells them to go, now, and that, "Pa is not." The seaplane has landed. The workers run into the depths of the island, no doubt to be hunted down and killed. Terrell and Maggie walk. Alpha calls after them, from the sea, but they keep walking. They sit under a tree on the island to await their death as the screen fades to white.

The ending of the film is reminiscent of the ending of *Carnal Knowledge* where Jonathan is listening to Louise, the prostitute, and the screen goes to white. But Jonathan does not realize that he is living out a fantasy. His is a spiritual death, death in life. In *The Day of the Dolphin*, Terrell is living in reality. He understands himself and the outer world. He may die physically, at the hands of the assassins, but he dies with real knowledge. George in *Who's Afraid of Virginia Woolf?* gained understanding and had hope, however slight, that things might be better between him and Martha. Benjamin in *The Graduate* got Elaine, new values, and some understanding, and had hope that their life together might be different from that of their parents. Yossarian in *Catch-22* gained insight, made his decision, and had hope that he could row to Sweden. Nevertheless, all these men still clung to some sort of hopeful fantasy and the fantasy increased from George, through Benjamin to Yossarian, to Jonathan, who became totally lost in his fantasy about himself and women. Terrell really has a fantasy at the beginning of the film (he is going to, for the good of the world, and not unlike Dr. Dolittle, talk to the animals), but at the conclusion of the film, he realizes that his dream cannot be totally realized. *The Day of the Dolphin* has a character who most realistically comes to terms with himself and the world. Terrell's realization is also a despairing one. The tragic ending especially sets the film apart from such "family" animal pictures as *Lassie*.

The ending of the film is typically a Nichols ending. The book was not just about Terrell's (Sevilla in the book) awakening to political intrigues. In the book, the dolphins are used not to try to blow up the President of the United States, but to plant an atomic device on a United States Naval Cruiser *Little Rock*, which does explode. This explosion is planned by a group of powerful men in order to have it look as if China planted the bomb. In this way, they think, the United States will have a reason to attack and destroy China with nuclear weapons, to insure "lasting peace." This is highly controversial matter for any movie. No wonder Nichols decided to use a presidential assassination. But, in the ending of the book, Sevilla (Terrell) has proof of the scheme, and the dolphins pull him and his party away from the island during the night. Sevilla has a chance of stopping the total nuclear war before the "ultimatum day" by presenting proof that it was not China that planted the device. The reader is left with the hope and the idea that Sevilla and his dolphins will explain the truth and save the world.

Nichols leaves no hope for Terrell to survive. He sits on his island as the screen fades to white (not unlike a nuclear explosion). All Nichols' films contain this element of despair, and his endings become more and more despairing in the progression from the first film, *Who's Afraid of Virginia Woolf?* to the sixth, *The Fortune.*

The Day of the Dolphin also clearly reflects the time in which it was made: political intrigue, assassinations, violence, and even Watergate. Note the many gates of water in the film—almost an abstract concept taking on a very concrete form.

The Day of the Dolphin followed *Carnal Knowledge* and displays several striking similarities to the earlier film. One is the despairing ending. In *Carnal Knowledge* Jonathan is defeated in his quest for a loving/sexual relationship with a woman. In *The Day of the Dolphin* Terrell is defeated in his quest with the dolphins for a better world. Both films contain dance motifs (as do the other Nichols' film, which will be discussed further in the last chapter). In *Carnal Knowledge* the skater dances and Susan dances with Jonathan and Sandy. In *The Day of the Dolphin* Alpha and Terrell swim/dance together as do Alpha and Beta, in what almost could be described as a ballet. Both films contain characters that look at the camera and talk directly to it.

The Day of the Dolphin contains many of the themes and elements of style that are found in other Nichols films: In many long, continuous takes the characters talk to each other; a motif of water runs symbolically through the film; there is the idea of symbolic drowning. Terrell cannot become a dolphin. As he is a man, he will drown if he stays with the dolphins in the sea for too long. The dolphins save the President from drowning (ultimately) but they can't save Terrell.

The environment reflects the characters' state of mind; the peaceful island is like Terrell, who is moving away from the civilization of man. This film has an angry major male figure who is searching for something. Terrell is fighting to continue his experiments and searching for a way to teach the dolphins to talk. A destructive woman interacts with the male; in this instance she is executive secretary Rome. The film contains a sterile, hostile environment in the Franklin Foundation. The characters are upper middle class and educated; part of the action takes place on Dr. Terrell's college-campus island, "The Terrell Marine Center." There is a turning point in the film, where the main male character changes, makes a decision, and moves to another psychological state. For Terrell, the turning point is his realization that his work may cause harm and his decision is to let the dolphins go. Religion is not mentioned in the film.

The idea that sex and love are separated, with sex destructive and love constructive, is not emphasized. However, the notion that a truly loving, sexual relationship for man is difficult, if not impossible, is present. The dolphins and not man may be the only ones to achieve a loving, sexual relationship. Maggie and Terrell are childless, and physical passion is not emphasized in their relationship, nor for that matter, in the relationship of the dolphins. But if the dolphins are, as Terrell claims, "instinct and energy," we can assume they have a sexual as well as a loving relationship. Alpha's sexual attempts with Maggie cease with the arrival of Beta. Of course, Terrell can touch the dolphins, but he cannot have sex with them; he can only love them.

And finally, there is the sad, pessimistic ending, where the male character has gained understanding, but not true freedom.

The Day of the Dolphin marked the formal end of the ten-year contract between Joseph E. Levine of Avco Embassy Films and Nichols. Levine said, "I feel very sad. In all those thirty-nine years since I started in films I never gave anybody carte blanche, but I gave Mike carte blanche. . . . I did it because I think he is a genius."[2]

Mr. Levine also said, "One of the things about 'Dolphin' which is a first. . . . We have received from abroad and from the United States and from NBC more money than our negative cost in guarantees—$8,450,000. That means, that before the film was even seen, there were guarantees covering more than its cost of $8,150,000."[3]

There are in reality scientists who do experiments with language and dolphins. Dr. John C. Lilly spent years trying to teach dolphins how to speak English. Dr. Lilly finally gave up his work on the grounds that it was cruel to take away the dolphins' freedom in the interest of research.[4] Terrell, at the conclusion of the film, lets the dolphins go free by sending them out to the sea. During the shooting of the film, Nichols said, "When we're done making the picture, we're going to let the dolphins go free. . . ."[5] After finishing the last shot, in the ocean off the island, the dolphins who played Alpha and Beta were freely swimming alongside the research boat back to shore, as they had done after countless shooting days before. Then, as if they knew that the shooting was finally finished and that they were no longer needed, of their own free will they turned and swam out to sea.

George C. Scott (Dr. Jake Terrell) and friend in The Day of the Dolphin.

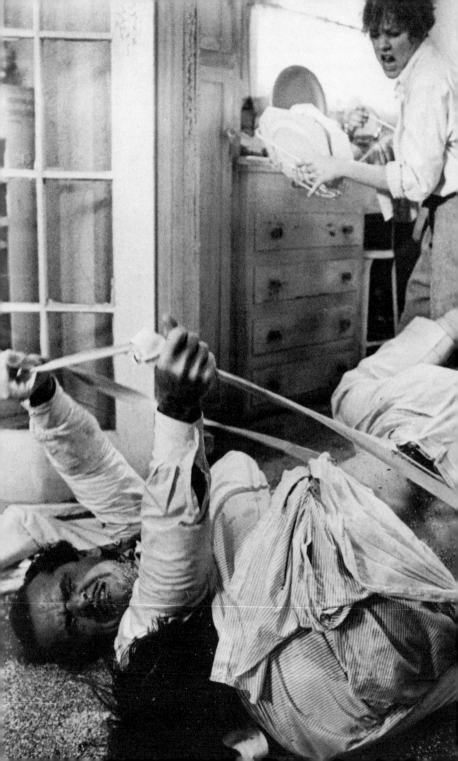

7

The Fortune

The Fortune is Mike Nichols' sixth film. It was written directly for the screen by Adrien Joyce, who also wrote *Five Easy Pieces*. During filming, Nichols was quoted as saying, "And this is the happiest I've ever been shooting a picture."[1]

The story is set in the 1920s. Nicky Stumpo (Warren Beatty) has convinced heiress-to-millions Fredricka Quintessa Biggard, called Freddie (Stockard Channing), that he wants to marry her as soon as his divorce is completed and that they should immediately run off to California together. Because of the Mann Act, which prohibited the transporting of a woman across state lines for immoral purposes, Nicky has convinced his friend Oscar Sullivan (Jack Nicholson) to marry Freddie and go with them to California. This "marriage of convenience" will last until Nicky gets his divorce. Oscar has been forced to cooperate. He has stolen fifteen hundred dollars from the bank in which he worked as a teller. Nicky has replaced the money but threatens to turn Oscar over to the authorities if he doesn't marry Freddie and go through with the plan. They go to California and all live together in a Spanish stucco court bungalow. Oscar becomes interested in Freddie's money, as Nicky is. When Freddie realizes that the men are more interested in the fortune she will inherit on her eighteenth birthday, she says that she will give it all to charity. Nicky and Oscar plan to kill her after her birthday so that Oscar will inherit her money. Then the two men plan to split the fortune. After a series of misadventures, they bungle the job. When Freddie learns about the attempt to murder her, she refuses to believe it and returns to the bungalow with Nicky and Oscar. The film ends.

In the first shot of the film we hear the music "I Must Be Dreaming," played in the style of the twenties. This song recurs throughout the film, and it is a comment on Freddie. As the song is heard,

129

the credits are superimposed over Freddie sneaking out of her home with a suitcase and getting into the car with Nicky.

In the first shot, then, we see two recurring elements in Nichols' work. The first relates to his style. It is the use of music as an element in the filmic symbol system to comment on the time and the action. The second relates to his recurring and complex theme of what happens to innocence confronted with experience. Freddie is the innocent dreamer who is being manipulated by Nicky, who is interested in her fortune.

That Nicky is a manipulator of both Freddie and Oscar echoes all the other manipulators we have seen in Nichols' films. Oscar himself later becomes manipulative as well. The two men also seem to possess a bit of innocence, or at least blindness to the real meaning of their actions.

Next in the film, Nicky picks up Oscar in the park. The dead leaves in the street are a visual symbol of the empty relationship that Freddie will be entering. Dead leaves were also emphasized on the campus in *Who's Afraid of Virginia Woolf?* and in *Carnal Knowledge*. Echoes of *Carnal Knowledge* are present too in the notion that here are two men who will become interested in one girl, as Jonathan and Sandy both became interested in Susan. Note the relationship to *Who's Afraid of Virginia Woolf?* with George and Nick (the same name, even) being attracted to Martha. One of the men in each of the films marries the woman. There are other interesting parallels. In *The Graduate* Benjamin and Mr. Robinson are both interested in Mrs. Robinson. In *The Day of the Dolphin* Alpha and Terrell are both interested in Maggie. In each case, one of the males is married. Five of Nichols' films have similar character relationships.

Even in the first few scenes of *The Fortune*, one can detect that it is a Nichols' film and that it is part of the larger pattern of his work. He is indeed an *auteur*, in whose work similar elements of theme and style recur over and over again.

Nicky, Oscar, and Freddie go to a justice of the peace, who marries Oscar and Freddie. At the end of the ceremony, Freddie kisses Nicky, has a drink, and faints. Nicky and she had been drinking from a flask in the car earlier. This sets up the idea that Freddie can't hold her liquor, which is important in one of the plots to kill her. Nichols also does the entire sequence without words (except for the song).

During the train and plane ride to California, Nicky treats Oscar selfishly. To avoid attracting attention to the trio, he doesn't want Oscar to play cards on the train. He subtly puts Oscar down when Oscar tells a story about "mouse beds" (what his mother used to call sanitary napkins) by saying he would have questioned what she did with them. Later during the plane ride, he isn't interested in Oscar's stories about flying. Oscar, upset by this, walks on the wings of the airplane. Nicky is furious. Thinking only of himself, he wonders how he would explain the situation if Oscar fell off. He does not think of Oscar's feelings. Oscar has to tell him, in fact, why he did it. Oscar says he feels left alone, ignored, like a fifth wheel. His feelings have been hurt. "After all," he says, "I'm here too."

Here are two examples of situations that start out to be comic, but instead turn out to be pathetic. The mouse bed story is supposed to be funny, but the put-down at the end when Nicky says he would have questioned what Oscar's mother did with the mouse beds, creates sympathy for Oscar. Freddie's fortune comes from sanitary napkins, but the viewer doesn't know this yet, so the story is left hanging with no connection. And it is not that funny to begin with.

The wing walking is funny because of its incongruity. But the motivation behind the wing walking is sad indeed: Oscar wants attention. And even when the humor turns to pathos, it is not of the Chaplinesque variety where the viewer can identify with Chaplin and share his humanity. With whom can the viewer really want to identify here? Probably not innocent, manipulated Freddie, or manipulating, cruel Nicky, or even crooked, lonely Oscar (although he seems the most likable of the trio). Real cruelty and hurt are going on here, and this cruelty and hurt will intensify. So *The Fortune*, although on the surface appearing to be a comedy, is underneath a despairing, painful tragedy. And this articulation of despair and pain, which we have seen in other Nichols' films, makes *The Fortune* a fine example of a Nichols film, but not a fine example of a comedy. Even if seen as farce, the callousness and selfishness of the characters are difficult to laugh at or with. In *The Graduate* we could side with Benjamin. In *The Fortune* it is difficult to side with anyone.

When, during the trip, Freddie had called her father, he had said that he was cutting her off from her inheritance. Nicky knows that she also has money coming from her mother on her eighteenth birthday, but he does not tell Oscar, another example of his manipulation. In fact, Oscar himself is somewhat innocent (even though he stole some money from the bank). He believes that Nicky loves Freddie, and only later realizes that he is in it for the money. The complex idea of innocence in Nichols' films will be discussed at length in the last chapter. Sufficient to note here that Oscar finally realizes what is happening and becomes involved later in a plot to kill Freddie.

Now, with music, come many shots of their first days in California. The trio rents a bungalow from Mrs. Gould (Florence Stanley). Nicky gets a job selling cars, which is important later in the plot. Freddie is seen trying to cook (she is really terrible at it) in a sailor suit. Oscar stays home and begins to be sexually attracted to Freddie, especially when she does exercises in front of him in her slip. Oscar buys her a little chick, and she is almost childlike in her affection for it. Her behavior may be another example of her innocence, or the little chick may also stand for the innocent Freddie (girls are often called "chicks"). The chick becomes a visual motif. As the chick grows up, so does Freddie.

Oscar begins to sport a mustache and to wear stylish clothes like Nicky. He is obviously imitating him, and during an outing in an automobile, they argue about this. The argument is like the preposterous ones that provided the plots for the Laurel and Hardy comedies, but again it is not very comic because of the biting words and anger of Nicky and Oscar. Freddie tries singing "Shaking the Blues Away," what she no doubt would like the car trip (and the shaking car) to do, but Nicky and Oscar continue to argue. Freddie has them stop the car and won't get back in. Finally they stop arguing when she threatens to call her father. They calm her down and Oscar rides separately in the back seat instead of up front with her and Nicky.

In the next scene, Freddie is dancing to the Victrola. She is dressed in Nicky's clothes. Oscar, looking very much like Nicky, is attracted to her and has her sit on his lap. A clever bit of verbal and visual symbolism occurs when Oscar asks for a peck on the cheek, or a kiss. Nichols has the camera focus on the chick pecking its feed. The use of the chick here could also indicate that Freddie (the little chick) sees this seduction innocently. Sexy Latin music on the Victrola echoes the sexy Latin music in Mrs. Robinson's seduction scene with innocent Benjamin in *The Graduate*. Oscar and Freddie go to the bedroom and make love.

It is important that Freddie is wearing men's clothes in this scene. We have seen her in a sailor suit, and here she was turned on not only by Oscar but by wearing Nicky's clothing. She told Oscar how, when she was a little girl, she once put on her brother's clothes and enjoyed walking on the streets at night. Also she goes by a boy's name "Freddie." This side of Freddie's character has an underlying sadness to it. Sexual implications aside, her behavior indicates that Freddie may be unhappy with herself as a woman. She wants to be someone else: a sailor, her brother, Nicky, any man.

Mrs. Gould, outside watering the plants (an interesting sexual metaphor with her hose shooting water), overhears Freddie and Oscar making love. Nicky comes home suddenly, and Oscar jumps out the bedroom window. (Nicky has told Mrs. Gould that Oscar is the husband and Nicky is the brother.) Nicky finds Freddie in bed alone, is turned on, and starts to make love to her. Mrs. Gould listens to this, too. Then Nicky finds a package of contraceptives that obviously belong to Oscar. When Oscar enters the house, Nicky confronts him with the contraceptives, and there is a terrible row. Freddie is very upset and joins in the fight. Freddie comments that they are several times more interested in each other than they are in her. Nicky says cruel things to Oscar about Freddie in regard to her money, such as "You think I've been breaking my hump here for nothing?" Oscar yells that he has discovered that Freddie is the "mouse-bed" heiress and that even though her father has disinherited her, she will get a fortune from her mother on her birthday. He screams about the money with which Nicky and she will go to Europe. He yells to Nicky that he, as the husband, has consummated the marriage, indicating that he did this for the money. Freddie says that "the scales have fallen from my eyes" (she is constantly talking in clichés from popular magazines and novels of the twenties), and that she realizes it is the money that is important to them and that they don't love her. She says that they have made her life a perfect hell. They only stop fighting after she says she is going to give all her money to charity. This confirms that the money is what they are interested in. In this scene, the men fighting with each other and Freddie throwing coffee and dishes at them may look funny but the scene again contains terrible cruelty and hurt.

Realizing that Freddie may indeed "get on a train" as she threatens, Nicky says he will forgive her for what happened between her and Oscar. He even calls her "Mumsy" and later, outside her locked door, says that whatever she wants to do (even giving all her money to charity) is absolutely fine with him.

While Nicky and Oscar are sitting at a gas station, Oscar talks about killing himself. Nicky misunderstands him and thinks he is planning to kill Freddie. They then plan to kill her after her birthday and make it look like an accident. Since Oscar, the husband, is the legal heir, he will inherit the money. He agrees to go halves with Nicky. However funny the antics of Oscar and Nicky may have been, this heartless and cruel plot dampens whatever comic spirit the film possesses—especially since the viewer's sympathies have been drawn first to Oscar and then primarily to Freddie. It is to Nichols' credit that the characters are three-dimensional and that the viewer can identify with them. This probably takes away from the film's comic, farcical effect, however.

The next scene is at Freddie's birthday party in a restaurant. It is done in one continuous shot with a moving camera. The music is again "I Must Be Dreaming." Freddie dances first with Nicky and then with Oscar. This dance motif, related to sex, can be found in all Nichols' feature films, almost like a trademark. In *Carnal Knowledge*, it is almost the same scene as in *The Fortune;* Susan jitterbugs first with Sandy and then with Jonathan. In *Who's Afraid of Virginia Woolf?* Martha dances at the roadhouse with Nick; in *The Graduate* the stripper dances on stage; in *Catch-22* Yossarian dances with Luciana; in *Carnal Knowledge* besides the jitterbug, Cindy dances alone and then with Jonathan; in *The Day of the Dolphin* Terrell and Alpha swim/dance, as do Alpha and Beta; and in *The Fortune* Freddie has also danced alone to the Victrola.

Freddie blows out the candles on a birthday cake, which indicates that this is her birthday and she has now turned eighteen. But the blowing out of the candles may have an ominous meaning, as when Terrell blew out the candles on the dolphin cake. In her relationship with Nicky and Oscar she may be facing her own death, both physical and spiritual.

Their first attempt to kill Freddie involves a good deal of farce. In order to buy a rattlesnake, Nicky dresses up in a ludicrous snake charmer outfit. Once he and Oscar have purchased a rattlesnake, they decide to test its effectiveness. They place it in the cage with the baby chicken, who is growing fast. Next morning, the chick is as healthy as ever, and the snake is dead. The comic sequence, however, has important implications. If the chicken symbolically stands for Freddie (a chick) it also may indicate to the viewer that she is "growing up" and will survive the "snakes," Nicky and Oscar.

In the next scene, Freddie serves an awful breakfast to Nicky and Oscar. She decided to cook a gourmet meal, including dessert, for breakfast. This is one of several indications that she is living in her own fantasy world. This scene also reinforces her innocence. She talks of her "doll-house days" when she served tea. She says her mother would have been pleased if she gave her money to her mother's charities. She acts like a little girl.

Nicky is upset, and Oscar encourages him to go through with their plans to kill Freddie and make it look like suicide. They plan to get her drunk, and when she passes out (that she can't hold her liquor was designed into the film earlier), drown her in the lily pond in front of the bungalow. Again note the theme of drowning that can be found in all Nichols' films to date.

Nicky tells Mrs. Gould that Freddie and Oscar have not been getting along and that she is depressed. He is setting up the suicide idea. Mrs. Gould says that with all the good things in life, she wonders why people can't get along better. This idea, although perhaps a cliché, is important to this film, for it points out the absurd and really depressing behavior of the trio, who seem hopelessly lost in problems of their own creation.

That night, the dance motif recurs as Oscar and Freddie dance while he and Nicky get her drunk. She sings "You've Got to See Mama Every Night Or You Can't See Mama At All," another use of an appropriate song to comment upon the action. If Nicky does not see Freddie every night (and it is also implied that he must be overly nice to her), then she may get on the train, so that he can't see her at all and perhaps may even go to jail on Mann Act Charges. When she passes out, they place her in the lily pond which looks like a giant birdbath. The birdbath idea relates to Freddie as the symbolic chick that they also tried to kill with the snake. Freddie, like the chick, foils the "snakes" by turning her head out of the water. Oscar and Nicky find the door locked so they can't get back into the bungalow. In a panic to get in, they throw a rock through their window. This awakens Mrs. Gould who finds Freddie and returns her to them.

Next—that same night while Freddie is still unconscious—Nicky and Oscar place her in a trunk and start out in their car, but it has a flat tire. They then carry the trunk to the used car lot, where they put it on top of a bus in the lot. (Nichols had set up the car lot [with the bus in the background] where Nicky works earlier in the film as part of the design.) They drive the bus onto a bridge over a river. They plan to throw Freddie into the river and make it look like suicide.

Here is one of the funniest parts of the movie, which evokes a 1920s slapstick comedy like Laurel and Hardy's *Two Tars*. The huge bus is near the middle of the bridge in solitude and Oscar and Nicky are taking the trunk off the top of the bus when they are interrupted by a car that tries to get around them. Nicky and Oscar place the trunk on the ground next to the bus. Then another car comes, then others, then a truck. Horns are honking and people are yelling. Nicky and Oscar put the trunk back on top of the bus. Freddie's shoes had fallen out of the trunk and Oscar puts the shoes in the bus. They push a car out of the way and go on. This scene works because of the marvelous incongruity of all those cars on a lonely bridge at night interrupting a murder, and also because it is basically visual comedy. This solitary bridge late at night—a perfect place for murder—suddenly becomes the center of a city-type traffic jam. This scene also emphasizes the hilarious bad luck of these would-be murderers.

They then go to the ocean and carry the trunk to the rocks at the edge. Nicky goes back to the bus for Freddie's shoes. A couple parks behind the bus to make love. When Oscar sees the car he panics and throws the trunk into the sea. Nicky says they must retrieve it, but they are interrupted by a fisherman (Scatman Crothers) who comes by to complain about all the trash people are throwing in the ocean these days. Nicky and Oscar leave to plan their story. Since Freddie is still in the trunk, they can hardly claim that she committed suicide. In his hurry to get away, Oscar backs the bus into the car where the couple are making love. The girl in the car says "Yes, yes," as if the crash were part of the lovemaking.

One can see here how well Nichols has designed these scenes. The shoes had fallen out of the trunk, so were put in the bus. When Oscar and Nicky carried the trunk to the ocean, they forgot the shoes, so Nicky went back for them. Thus, the shoes become the motivation for Nicky to leave Oscar with the trunk. The car with the lovers becomes the motivation for Oscar to throw the trunk in the bay. The fisherman becomes the motivation that stops the men from getting the trunk back. And the car with the lovers is used again when the bus hits them, almost like a punctuation mark to end the scene.

The bus pulls away, and Nicky and Oscar, in panic, argue about what to do next. They then turn around to go back to the beach. It is sunrise. Now in daylight, with "I Must Be Dreaming" playing sadly on the soundtrack, Freddie climbs out of the trunk that has washed up on the beach. She walks up to the road and a man named John (Tom Newman), who appropriately sports a mustache as Nicky and Oscar do, picks her up in his car. When she asks where she is, John says "Long Beach." She can't remember what happened to her since she first passed out at the bungalow.

The car passes the bus going in the other direction. Nicky and Oscar see the empty trunk on the beach. Perhaps they believe that Freddie has been washed out of it. The trunk is washed around in the sea as the men examine it.

Nicky and Oscar return to the bungalow and plan to wait and see what happens. The stripes on Nicky's bathrobe look like bars on a prison uniform, a good visual symbol. When the police come to investigate the stolen bus, Oscar is so frightened that he blurts out something about putting her in the trunk. The police are then very interested.

John and Freddie are at John's place. John (who is appropriately enough a barber who may clip Freddie out of her money and trim her as well) is kissing Freddie. She wants him to help her think up a story (about what she did during the night) and says that she should go home and face the music, as she thinks that Nicky and Oscar must be beside themselves.

At the police station, Oscar confesses in great detail. While this is going on Freddie has decided to run away with John. She and John go to the bungalow to pick up her things. John says she must leave Nicky a note. The police and Oscar and Nicky return to the outside of the bungalow where Oscar begins to reenact the crime. When Freddie sees them outside, she thinks that Oscar and Nicky have called the police because they are worried about her being missing. I feel that she is so immature that she decides to leave with John rather than face the two men. Nichols cuts between the police outside and Freddie inside. John and Freddie sneak out the back way as the police and Oscar and Nicky go in the front way. Freddie forgets her chicken, and goes to the garage for it. Oscar and the police see Freddie running with the chicken to John's car. The police catch up to her, and the chief detective tells her about the plots to kill her.

The ending of the picture is remarkable visually and an example of Nichols' excellent command of the film medium. Nicky and Oscar walk toward the camera. There is a cut so that the viewer sees from their point of view, and the camera moves in from a long shot of Freddie, sitting on the running board of the police car, the detective talking with her, and the chicken (now grown up like Freddie) on the ground in front of them. As the detective begins to tell about the murder attempt, the music "I Must Be Dreaming" again plays happily on the soundtrack so his words cannot be heard. The camera continues to move to a close-up shot of Freddie's face. Freddie looks hurt and sad. As the detective finishes his story of how Nicky and Oscar tried to kill her, Freddie looks directly at the camera (a Nichols trademark) and says, "Oh, no, I would never believe that in a million years." Nichols cuts to Nicky and Oscar and then back to Freddie's face. The last shot is continuous until the end of the film. The camera begins a slow ninety-degree pan from her face around to the street where John's car pulls away and then to the trio walking toward the bungalow. Oscar, Freddie, and Nicky walk toward the bungalow together carrying her suitcase and chicken and go into the bungalow. "I Must Be Dreaming" is now sung. Mrs. Gould comes out and begins to water the yard, and then sneaks behind the side of the bungalow to listen. The credits roll.

The ending is certainly appropriate for a Nichols film. Freddie remains unable to break out of her relationship with the two men. She remains in her fantasy world. "I would never believe that in a million years," she says. She will continue to live the death-in-life (she said they have made her life pure hell) or if she isn't careful, she will have a real death at the hands of Oscar and Nicky. She is as dead as Jonathan at the end of *Carnal Knowledge* and Terrell at the end of *The Day of the Dolphin*.

Stockard Channing said about the ending, "In a sense, these people all kind of belong together—they're married to each other. They're all they have, and Freddie just doesn't want to leave the two men; like people in a real marriage, she'll tolerate even physical violence. When they stay together at the end, they may try to kill her again, but she'll keep bouncing back."[2]

Nichols has said: "I'm so confused by other people's responses to my movies. To me, the people in *Virginia Woolf* have a good marriage. They want more for the other one than for themselves. It reminds me of the end of *The Fortune;* the men treat Freddie badly, but, despite that they're friends—they're bound together, the three of them. . . ."[3]

There is another interpretation to the ending, but it is not reinforced by the film itself. Freddie may realize that the men have tried to kill her; but she has grown fond of Nicky and Oscar and so decides not to tell on them so that they will not be prosecuted by the police. As soon as the police leave she may leave the men. But, by ending the film where he did, Nichols leaves the impression that the trio will continue to live their unhappy, death-in-life. And this is consistent with the endings of other Nichols films. Freddie may have gained insight (even though she rejects it) but will not become free. It is a despairing ending and certainly not a comic one.

Freddie's actions are believable. Assuming her mother is dead, she has grown up with her father and her brother. Thus she really knows only men and not what women are like (how ironic that she is a sanitary napkin heiress). She even likes to wear men's clothing. Nicky and Oscar are to her like her father and her brother. She trusts them and goes back to continue living out this psychological pattern.

The ending is consistent with an idea found in other Nichols' films, the notion that a character can't really break out of his or her self-imposed prison. They may try, but they really can't make it. There may be a glimmer of hope that they have all been changed by their experience, and will live happily ever after, but one doubts it. Throughout this film, the main characters consistently fail at what they are trying to do. For example, Freddie can't cook; Oscar and Nicky can't kill Freddie; they just cannot cope with anything.

Andrew Sarris said about *The Graduate,* "*The Graduate* is moving precisely because its hero passes from a premature maturity to an innocence regained, and idealism reconfirmed."[4] In Freddie's case, innocence has met with experience, but in a strange way remains. Freddie seems as innocent at the beginning of the film as she does at the end since, unlike Benjamin in *The Graduate,* she does not have a "premature maturity" nor does she really profit from what she experiences. She rejects the knowledge that the men have tried to kill her. She remains living out her psychological pattern in fantasy. She is the one who "must be dreaming." Likewise, Nicky and Oscar seem innocent in the way that they do not seem to understand the terrible hurt, both psychological and physical, that they are inflicting.

Nichols has said, *"The Fortune* is a leap into extremes of behavior—last resorts. It's about people so innocent that they don't know when you kill someone she dies. It's like kids playing bang-bang."[5]

The Fortune does not move the viewer as *The Graduate* does. It offers no insight, no real rebellion against a set of values, no real losing of or subsequent regaining of innocence. The characters in *The Fortune* don't really change psychological states; their behavior just becomes more bizarre.

Stockard Channing said:

. . . It is partially a story about shifting roles. The mousebed is a symbol of what men don't know about women, and it parallels the situation in the movie. If the boys had gone along with Freddie, she'd have given them anything, but instead they try to wrest it away from her. It's about role playing between men and women. . . . The symbolism is always there. It's important that the fortune is from Freddie's mother, from the maternal side—there's a double meaning in that, because she has the burden of the fortune and the burden of the menstrual cycle, too. Mike said in rehearsal that it's like Freddie is the fortune and they miss it completely. She's like the goose laying the golden eggs, and they miss it. It's like raping Mother Earth—you can go on and on like that.[6]

Note the "role playing between men and women" and how this idea can also be found in *Carnal Knowledge.*

Stanley Kauffman senses the despairing feeling of the film, although he thinks it ends merrily: "The fact that it all ends merrily doesn't help. Death is often an element of farce, on the edge or as a threat to central characters, but the serious effort of one central character, let alone two, to kill another is not farcical. In farce we laugh at the protagonist's frustrated attempts to do something we want him to succeed at. That's flatly impossible here. And it makes the reconciled ending even a bit distasteful."[7]

Nichols presents us with a comic environment, but in that environment events that are definitely not funny happen. In *Newsweek,* Paul D. Zimmerman states well the feeling of the film: ". . . he creates a comic *Chinatown,* a moral wasteland of mean motives and faithless acts in which comedy can't flourish."[8]

Some critics saw *The Fortune* as very funny. One critic called it "the best motion picture of the last twenty-five years."[9] Vincent Canby in the *New York Times* called it "very funny, maniacally scatterbrained."[10] Nichols himself said "I meant *The Fortune* to be a small, happy, funny movie. I didn't mean it to be a monument, a major final utterance. Movies come in all sizes. The whole trick is not to take yourself too seriously and on the other hand, not to throw yourself away."[11]

With *The Fortune,* Nichols set up a comic climate, but created a sad and despairing film with comic moments. Within this frame of reference, it is a good film. It is part of Nichols' particular vision that can be seen in his other films as well, though audiences may find this frame of reference unacceptable.

The Fortune contains themes and elements of style found in all Nichols films. There are the many long, continuous takes in which the characters talk to each other. For example, Oscar's mouse-bed story to Nicky and the gas station discussion of Freddie's murder. The scenes at the lily pond, on the bridge, and in the ocean continue a motif of water which runs symbolically through the film. Nichols again uses the symbolic drowning motif, where Freddie is first threatened with the lily pond, then the river, and finally floats in the ocean in a trunk. The environment reflects the characters' state of mind: the messy house, the unappetizing food. Nichols' angry male figure searching for something is Nicky, although Oscar is also searching. They are searching for money and happiness. Freddie, although a female, has a male name and enjoys wearing men's clothing. She is also searching, for love and happiness. She also may be the destructive woman who interacts with the males, but she is unintentionally destructive. The sterile, often hostile environment is seen in the bungalow complex run by Mrs. Gould. The characters are middle class and educated, but no college campus appears this time. There is a turning point in the film where the characters make a decision, but they don't seem really to change psychological states.

Nicky's decision is to murder Freddie. Oscar's decision is to murder Freddie. Freddie remains a dreamer, and her decision is to reject the detective's story and return to Nicky and Oscar.

The idea that sex and love are separated, with sex destructive and love constructive, appears in the film. Coupled with this is the notion that a truly loving, sexual relationship is not possible. Nicky is getting a divorce; his first relationship with a woman did not work out. He does not love Freddie but has sex with her. Oscar likes Freddie and buys her a chick, but later it seems that this is part of a seduction in order to get her to have sex with him. During this seduction, while he is trying to persuade her to kiss him, he reminds her that he bought her a chick. John, the barber, seems sexually interested in Freddie. Freddie may think she has a loving, sexual relationship with Nicky, yet she goes to bed with Oscar. One of the things that makes *The Fortune* so despairing is that no one seems really to love or show concern for anybody in a meaningful way. Nicky and Oscar just use Freddie, a person who has real emotional problems.

In the sad, pessimistic ending at least one of the characters, Freddie, is offered knowledge but by rejecting it fails to gain freedom.

8

"Family"

TWO YEARS AFTER the release of *The Fortune*, Mike Nichols has not yet started another film, but he has kept busy. He directed two hits on Broadway, *Comedians* and *Streamers*, in 1976. He also produced the television series, "Family," that year.

"Family" is a Mike Nichols Production, shot on film for television at the 20th Century-Fox studios. It is important in this analysis because Mike Nichols developed this project; it was his vision that guided it, and it represents a venture into a new media related to film.

Nichols did not direct any of the episodes. As with his theatrical films, he surrounded himself with very talented people. According to David Cuthbert, *"Family* began . . . as an unlikely project of Spelling-Goldberg, the production team more widely noted for slam-bang shoot-em-up projects like *Starsky and Hutch* and *SWAT*. It's creator was Jay Presson Allen, whose stage and screen credits include adaptations of *Cabaret* and *The Prime of Miss Jean Brodie*. Her pilot script languished on an ABC shelf until it was rescued by Mike Nichols, who had been asked by ABC to tackle a TV production—*any* TV production."[1]

Also working on the series were executive producers Aaron Spelling and Leonard Goldberg, director Mark Rydell, as executive consultant, producers/writers Nigel and Carol Evan McKeand, and directors Robert Hartford-Davis, John Erman, Glenn Jordon, Richard Kinon, Edward Parone, and others.

Television series films are different from theatrical films. An hour-long episode must be provided each week. The necessity for so many hours of film make it almost impossible for one director to direct all the shows. There is usually little time for thoughtful contemplation. Committee collaboration is usually increased on a tele-

145

"Family" portrait.

ɔurtesy of 20th Century-Fox Studios

vision series, and the role of producer/coordinator is most important.

The television drama is more restricted than the theatrical film in certain ways. Where the theatrical film usually runs continuously anywhere from an hour and a half to three hours and does not have to end at any particular time, television programs are usually limited to definite time blocks: thirty minutes, an hour, an hour and a half, two hours. Producers have to allow for commercial breaks.

Theatrical films, because of the big screen, may employ shots of many sizes and are not bound to include much verbal material; television, on the other hand, because of the small screen, is a close-up to medium-shot medium, and much of the plot is carried by words. Television films and theatrical films, then, are two different mediums. They share elements of the same symbol system, but have their own unique strengths and limitations. "Family," although shot on film, is designed by Nichols for television. It is a psychological drama in which characters are continually talking with or about each other in medium shots or close-ups.

"Family" does occasionally deal with controversial subjects, but they are handled in a mature, tasteful way. The subjects are not exploited. As in Nichols' theatrical films, they are handled with discretion, responsibility, and artistry. The films are not glorified soap operas, but domestic dramas. They are well written, well directed, and contain believable, three-dimensional characters. Plots have dealt with adultery, divorce, illness, homosexuality, and alcoholism, as well as responsibility, growing up, honesty, friendship, loneliness, death, love, coping, and taking chances. "Family" provides a look at a contemporary family coping with problems in a mature, responsible way.

The show is about a family living in Pasadena. As in other Nichols films, they are upper middle class, well off financially, and educated. The father, Doug Lawrence (James Broderick), is a lawyer. The mother, Kate Lawrence (Sada Thompson), is a housewife who also attends college and studies music. There are two daughters and a son. Nancy Douglas Maitland (Meredith Baxter-Birney) is in her twenties, divorced, and has a child, Timmy. Willie Lawrence (Gary Frank) is eighteen. He dropped out of high school, but after taking an equivalency exam, graduated and works for a photographer (photographs are a recurring visual motif in the shows). Lititia Lawrence, called "Buddy" (Kristy McNichol), is thirteen, goes to school, and skateboards. All the children live at home, and all face numerous trials and problems. I have chosen two early episodes in the series as examples of the kind of situations employed and the handling of them.

The first is "Thursday's Child," first aired in April, 1976. Nancy wants to have her child christened "Timmy." Timmy was the name of her little brother who drowned in an accident five years before. Although her family has discouraged her, Buddy had insisted on going on a boat trip with her father, Willie and Timmy. When the boat overturned accidentally, Timmy was drowned but Buddy was rescued. She feels responsibility for his death and always wears a cap that he wore. Buddy objects to having Nancy's baby named Timmy and can't cope with the christening. After the christening, Buddy's father takes her to the cemetery to say goodbye to the dead Timmy and assures her that his death was an accident. She cries and accepts Timmy's name for the new baby. Her father comforts her with a line from a nursery rhyme; she was born on Thursday and "Thursday's child has far to go." Later, she tells the live Timmy to have a good life.

The second episode is "A Special Kind of Loving," first aired in March, 1976. Buddy is having trouble diving into a pool. She is the only girl in her group who cannot make this dive. She is terrified of sticking to the bottom. She wants someone to pull her up. In a parallel story, Willie becomes involved with Salina McGee, a young woman who works at Nature's Cupboard, a health food restaurant. Salina, unmarried, is pregnant (has someone else's baby in her "Nature's Cupboard") but does not tell Willie. Willie does not come to help Buddy dive, as he is busy seeing Salina. Buddy, angry at Willie for not helping her, lies to him and says she dived. Buddy overhears at a clinic that Salina is three months pregnant, and tells Willie. Buddy dives into the pool later, thinking she is alone. She does swim by herself but Willie catches her hand. He lends her a hand, as Buddy has symbolically lent Willie a hand by telling him the truth about Salina. After talking with Kate (Willie's mother), Salina decides to have the baby, not an abortion. Willie and Salina come to an understanding, and Willie tells her that he loves her.

The series tries to be as human and as realistic as possible and is very carefully structured. Even the sets for the interior of the house have been carefully designed to look real. Some elements in Nichols' theatrical films can also be found in this series, in the episodes described and in certain other episodes. Kate (the mother) and Nancy attend college, and many times scenes take place on the campus. A character trying to save himself from drowning and the fear of symbolic drowning (Timmy has drowned; Buddy was afraid to dive) recur. Men are interested in Nancy, a divorcée (shades of all the other two-men, one-woman relationships found in Nichols' films). And, most clearly, the characters are bound together, unable to break out of the "family." Two of the children are able to (and probably should) leave home to make a life of their own, but they do not seem to want to. Willie is "looking for himself," searching for something, like the typical Nichols male figure, but as long as he stays home, he probably won't find himself.

The characters possess great insight. They are flexible, and especially the parents seem to understand themselves and their children. Buddy is also extremely insightful.

It is difficult really to know exactly how much influence Nichols has had in this series. But the consistent elements and the quality of the production suggest that it has been considerable.

"Family" was first a mini-series of six programs, beginning in March, 1976. It was then picked up by ABC for a full season of programs in the 1976–77 season. It was the first show that ABC renewed for the 1977–78 season. With his brilliant "Family," Nichols has now fully demonstrated his ability as an artist in theater, in film, and in television. Since launching this project, he presented the Broadway musical *Annie* in 1977. According to the *Hollywood Reporter*, the picture version of *Annie* "will be helmed by Bob Evans and Mike Nichols" if the motion picture rights to *Annie* can be negotiated with Paramount.[2] He also directed the play *The Gin Game* on Broadway in 1977.

9

The Nichols Touch

ONE FILM NICHOLS DECIDED not to direct was *The Exorcist*. He said, "I tried to be tempted by it and I tried very hard to regret it when I turned it down. I asked Elaine (May) to help me try to regret it—all that money lost. She said, 'Don't regret it. If you had made the movie, it wouldn't have made all that money.' The point of the story, you can't fake something. If it's not your material, you can't do it."[1]

I think that this statement is very true. I assume Nichols is attracted to projects that are in line with his personal vision. If he had made *The Exorcist*, it would have been a very different film, probably colored by the themes and elements of style found in his other films.

He has made another statement, which is right to the point, "I'm not sure my movies need to be linked together, but in my mind they're almost the same picture over and over."[2]

This confirms my opinion that Nichols is indeed what the French call an *auteur*, the author of his work. His films bear the stamp of his personality and like many great artists, he seems to be producing the same work over and over again. His films are part of a complex, profound mosaic. His personal vision, his themes, and his style can be seen as unifying elements in his films taken as a whole.

Geoffrey Nowell-Smith has summed up the *auteur* theory as it is normally presented today: "One essential corollary of the theory as it has been developed is the discovery that the defining characteristics of an author's work are not necessarily those which are most readily apparent. The purpose of criticism thus becomes to uncover behind the superficial contrasts of subject and treatment a hard core of basic and often recondite motifs. The pattern formed by those motifs . . . is what gives an author's work its particular structure, both defining it and distinguishing one body of work from another."[3]

151

In the preceding chapters, I have discussed many differences and similarities in Nichols' films. Now I would like to probe more deeply into a few of the underlying important similarities.

Nichols presents his vision through laughter in many of his films, perhaps not to have us turn away in horror. Without the comedy, many of his films would become almost too painful to watch and perhaps too painful for even Nichols to create. While discussing the distinction between comedy and tragedy, Nichols said, "I hate and refuse to make the distinction. Life is not a comedy and life is not a tragedy, whatever the hell it is. It may be both. What the director is saying to his audience is, 'This happened to me; did it happen to you, too?' Metaphorically, almost always, not literally. . . . 'Do you experience things as I do? Is it like that for you?' . . . The first question is the one the audience asks: 'Why are you telling me this?' And you have to know why. And then you ask the audience a queston, the only question I know to ask. You say, 'Is this like your life? Does this remind you of something? Does it seem familiar at all?' If you're lucky, it does."[4]

In his films, Nichols presents a deep, disturbing, coherent view of the human condition and poses questions about it for which there are no easy answers.

Nichols' films seem to be based on an honest and profound awareness of the tragic nature of the human condition. One theme that relates to this appears in all his films. It is the idea of real or symbolic drowning and is connected with the image of water. In *Who's Afraid of Virginia Woolf?* George drinks too much and Martha calls him a drowning man. Benjamin in *The Graduate* drowns among objects and symbolically in his swimming pool. In *Catch-22* Yossarian fears drowning in the ocean and is seen going underwater clutching at the nurse's uniform. In *Carnal Knowledge* Jonathan takes numerous showers (perhaps to "drown" feelings), jumps in the pool, and finds water turned to ice. Terrell in *The Day of the Dolphin* can't swim with his dolphins forever or become one or he will drown. Freddie in *The Fortune* is dumped in a lily pond and thrown in the ocean. In "Family" Timmy drowns and Buddy overcomes her fear of the water. This drowning imagery is central to Nichols' films and may go beyond to other aspects of the man as well.

Nichols' production company is called Icarus Productions. In mythology, Icarus was the son of Daedalus, who built the labyrinth on the island of Crete. He lost favor with King Minos after the minotaur, who lived in the labyrinth, was slain. Daedalus and Icarus were imprisoned on the island by King Minos. To escape back to Greece, Daedalus built wings out of feathers and wax for his son and himself. Daedalus told Icarus to follow him, but warned him not to fly too high. While Icarus was following his father, he flew too high and the sun melted his wings. Icarus fell into the sea and was drowned.

The Icarus myth may have important implications in Nichols' private life. At eight years old, he traveled to America by ship. His father had left Nazi Germany and then sent for Mike and his brother. Like Icarus, young Mike followed his father to escape from a hostile environment. Also Nichols first followed his doctor father by enrolling in medical school, but dropped out to become an actor and an improvisational comedian. Later he became a stage and film director. Of course, Nichols became a great success and did not symbolically drown. Yet Nichols' vision as seen through his films is consistent with the myth of Icarus. He still expresses fears of "flying too high." He seems to feel that more characters symbolically perish than live happily ever after.

There is another important theme that runs through Nichols' films. His characters seem to carry with them into the present the burden of the past. Even in his earlier skits with Elaine May, his characters would say something like, "I had a middle class background. No relating to my parents." One of his most popular skits deals with a grown man whose mother reduces him to infantilism while he talks with her on the phone. In *Who's Afraid of Virginia Woolf?* George talks about accidentally killing his father; in *The Graduate* Benjamin fights to free himself from his parents' values; in *Catch-22* Yossarian inherits a war and the insane structures of military life; in *Carnal Knowledge* Jonathan and Sandy go to college for family reasons and inherit destructive stereotypes of men and women; in *The Day of the Dolphin*, when Alpha tries to learn the language of man, he is suddenly drawn into intrigues which result from a history he knows nothing about; in *The Fortune* Freddie must deal with the fortune accumulated by her parents; in "Family" the characters all appear tied down by their relationship. In various ways, the characters try to place the past in perspective so that they may live comfortably in the present.

But Nichols seems to be working toward some way of coping. He

has said, in relation to *The Graduate*, ". . . a lot of us have the
fantasy of breaking out, of dropping everything, of disappearing
with that one girl, and extending a certain feeling forever, or taking
the moment—let's say those three hours of your sitting with a girl
and she's holding your foot and you think: 'I would like her to go on
holding my foot for the rest of my life. I don't want to go out and
work. I don't want to go to dinner with those people I'm supposed to
meet. I don't want to do anything. I want my life to be *this* and
nothing else.' It's something everybody knows. And this fantasy of
breaking through everything and living for that is a very powerful
one. I think it can't be done. I think a lot of people, myself included,
wish to God it could be done. And that's what the end [of *The
Graduate*] means to me. That I'm moved by somebody who wants to
try to do it and I'm pulling for them. But I don't know if they can
make it."[5]

This statement can apply to all his feature films. In his first three
films, as we have seen, there seems to be a bit of hope that the main
characters "can make it," although really not much. George may
have changed his and Martha's relationship, Benjamin may have a
life with Elaine different from that of his parents, and Yossarian may
get to Sweden. But the structure and imagery of these films suggest
that there is only a wisp of hope that they will.

In Nichols' last three films, there seems to be no hope at all for
any of the main characters to save themselves, or in Nichols' words,
to "break out." In *Carnal Knowledge* Jonathan remains in his fantasy
world about women; in *The Day of the Dolphin*, with the dolphins
gone, Terrell waits for death; in *The Fortune* Freddie returns to her
former relationship with Nicky and Oscar. Even the characters in
the television series "Family" seem destined to remain together
until the series ends, but whether this is a hopeless situation remains to be seen.

The characters in each of the films, however, have their beautiful
moments, the "certain feeling" Nichols talks about, although they
can't extend it and "break out." Some examples of such moments
can be found in each film: the loving feelings between George and
Martha; Benjamin and Elaine's courtship; Yossarian's feelings for
Luciana and his close friends; the friendships in *Carnal Knowledge*,
especially between Jonathan and Susan and between Jonathan and
Bobbie before their relationships deteriorate; the love between Terrell and the dolphins; the good times shared by Oscar, Nicky and

Freddie; and in "Family" the love that sees the characters through crises.

Each of the main characters also does noble, loving deeds. George tries to save himself and Martha; Benjamin tries to save himself and Elaine; Yossarian tries to save himself and is loyal to his friends by not compromising himself and by respecting the painful memory of Snowden; Jonathan does not tell Sandy about his relationship with Susan or fight him for her; Terrell tries to teach dolphins to talk and saves the President; Freddie does not turn Nicky and Oscar over to the police. Although Nichols' characters are unable to "break out," they are sometimes able to do significant things, gain understanding, make lasting friendships, move to different psychological states, help others who are also trapped.

Nichols' films present a universe where there is little possibility of combined loving/sexual relationships; where people often do not perceive when they trample on others' feelings; where people often act according to their own selfish, aggressive, and manipulative motives; where they are often hurt and angry; and where they have few beautiful moments to try to extend. It may be argued that many of Nichols' characters are as happy as possible in such a universe.

Nichols has said about his films, "They're all about friendship and making the best of a rough situation and not coming to any final decision about other people or oneself. . . ."[6]

Nichols' characters also "draw the line and will go no farther." George will not continue the destructive games with Martha; Benjamin will not settle for his parents' values; Yossarian will not accept the horrors around him; Jonathan will not destroy his friendship with Sandy to fight for Susan; Terrell will not passively let his dolphins be used to kill the President; Freddie will not turn Oscar and Nicky over to the police. Characters in "Family" similarly draw the line in various episodes.

The theme of sacrifice for one's friends is frequently evident. George stays with Martha and tries to help; Benjamin is saving himself but also will try to save Elaine from her living death; Yossarian will not "cop out" on his friends; Jonathan does not tell Sandy about his relationship with Susan; Terrell sends Alpha and Beta away so that they will not be hurt; Freddie stays with Oscar and Nicky; the "Family" stays together and helps one another.

To summarize and synthesize some of the themes found in Nichols' films, we see angry main characters searching for something; domineering, often destructive women; sterile, often hostile environments in an upper middle class, educated subculture; the repeated idea that sex and love are separated, with sex destructive and love constructive, coupled with the idea that a truly loving, sexual relationship which lasts is perhaps not possible. Each film has a turning point where the characters make painful decisions. The sad, pessimistic endings show that the characters may have gained understanding, but have not gained true freedom.

And, as mentioned earlier, Nichols' films all deal with a concept of innocence. However cruel George and Martha are to each other in *Who's Afraid of Virginia Woolf?* their fantasies about an imaginary child and the games of abuse they play with each other are almost childlike. Through the evening, they begin to experience reality. In *The Graduate* Benjamin is innocent (he hasn't graduated into life yet), as is Elaine. Through experience, Benjamin is enlightened, as is Elaine. Yossarian in *Catch-22* is buffeted around, regarded as crazy. He is innocent—as symbolized by his nakedness at the awards ceremony—until he confronts his experiences and discovers their true meaning. Certainly Jonathan, Sandy, and even Susan in *Carnal Knowledge* are innocent. They are in college and virgins. Their experiences and the way in which they perceive and react to them are important in imparting the suggestion that "carnal knowledge" may not be worth the loss of innocence. In *The Day of the Dolphin* Alpha is certainly innocent until Terrell begins his teachings, and Terrell himself is innocent about the political scheming going on around him. In *The Fortune*, Freddy, Oscar, and Nicky are all comically innocent (they may never really lose their innocence since they never seem at all conscious of the depravity of their plots). In "Family" various levels of innocence are stripped way as the members of the Lawrence family experience life. For Nichols, innocence does not seem to be a survival characteristic. (Thus the persistent innocence of the characters in *The Fortune* is ominous and may also have alienated audiences through the threat to their own illusions about innocence.)

Some of the characters regain their innocence, so to speak: Benjamin, Elaine, Sandy, and Freddie. The majority of them, however, lose it and come, with masks off, face to face with themselves and Nichols' sobering reality.

The universe Nichols creates is a rough one, where beautiful moments may be what are really important. Friendships, even though imperfect, also are seen in a hostile, corrupt, selfish, and cold inner and outer world. If there is little hope for the characters to attain true happiness, the ray of hope that shines into all the despair in the Nichols filmic world may be beautiful moments in friendship. Friendships often endure although at times one of the character's friends may act badly toward him. Martha sleeps with Nick, but George remains her friend; Elaine dates and marries Carl, but Benjamin remains her friend; friends act badly toward Yossarian, but he remains decent and true to them. Jonathan betrays Sandy with Susan, but Sandy remains his friend when he finds out; Alpha bites Maggie and won't talk while with Beta, but Terrell remains his friend; Freddie remains friends with Nicky and Oscar, who have tried to kill her; in "Family" characters betray each other occasionally but remain friends. So love and friendships are important in Nichols' difficult universe and they can exist between men and women (clearly the emphasis in *Who's Afraid of Virginia Woolf?* and *The Graduate*), men and men (the emphasis in *Carnal Knowledge, The Fortune,* and *Catch-22*), men and animals *(The Day of the Dolphin),* and family members ("Family").

Perhaps friendships cannot last. Perhaps they are transitory, like the beautiful moments. In *Carnal Knowledge* Susan tells Jonathan that she will always be his friend. Jonathan, who has been terribly hurt by her, replies, "Jesus, Susan, I hope not."

If the characters in Nichols' films can't really "extend the feeling" or "break out," then the despairing endings are understandable.

But perhaps there is more hope in Nichols' film than I have indicated, if one looks at hope a certain way. When asked if there was hope for George and Martha at the end of *Who's Afraid of Virginia Woolf?* Nichols said, "Hope for people is a confusing idea for me, because I'm not sure where hope lies. If hope means Martha will start coming downstairs in a pretty little dress for breakfast and make interesting dishes for George and ask what happened in his classroom, there is no hope of that. But if hope is being alive and touching each other and not being alone and having it really, really mean something when you make love, then there's hope for them."[7]

If I were to sum up the meaning I find in Nichols' films thus far, it would be that life is made up of beautiful moments with friends who love each other, but because of the inner and outer human condition, those moments cannot endure.

There are other recurring motifs that are related to what I see as

Nichols' world view. One is the dance, which in one sense is a rigid, formalized social ritual, while in another, it is the expression of frenzy and passion. In *Who's Afraid of Virginia Woolf?* Martha dances with Nick; in *The Graduate* the stripper dances as Elaine is humiliated; in *Catch-22* Yossarian and Luciana dance; in *Carnal Knowledge* Susan jitterbugs with Jonathan and Sandy and the skater dances; in *The Day of the Dolphin* Terrell and the dolphins do a kind of swim-dance; in *The Fortune* Freddie dances with Oscar and Nicky; and in "Family," in one episode, Buddy tries to get Nancy to teach her to dance. In all social and instinctual forces contend.

Another motif is that of the human head, in close-up, either floating in the frame or talking to the camera. It may relate to Nichols' interest in selfish or introspective characters. Recall the giant close-ups of Martha and George in *Who's Afraid of Virginia Woolf?*; Benjamin's head floating through the party in *The Graduate*; Yossarian's head coming into frame in the "Help the bombardier" scenes in *Catch-22*; Susan walking into the college mixer and Jonathan addressing the camera in *Carnal Knowledge*; DeMilo and Mahoney's heads in the Franklin Foundation office, and the dolphin's eye looking at the viewers in the beginning of *The Day of the Dolphin*; Freddie looking at the camera when she says she doesn't believe the story about the attempted murder in *The Fortune*; and numerous close-ups on the small television screen in "Family."

I mentioned before the many long continuous takes in which characters talk to each other, reminiscent of the early Nichols and May skits. Nichols, like Antonioni, is more concerned with what is in the frame than with fancy editing. He holds his shots a long time, forcing the audience to become involved with what is happening in the shot, to read it, and to participate in it.

Music and songs play a major role in setting the time period and commenting on the action, not just creating "moods" in the audience. Nichols avoids conventional background music.

Who's Afraid of Virginia Woolf?, *The Graduate*, *Carnal Knowledge*, and "Family" all take place in part on a college campus, and *The Day of the Dolphin* takes place in part at a research facility. Nichols uses the learning centers as a backdrop to examine the lives of his characters. Yet real learning for his characters does not seem to come from the colleges themselves, but from relationships between the characters or from elsewhere.

All Nichols' theatrical films are from the point of view of male characters. In *Who's Afraid of Virginia Woolf?* the point of view is George's; in *The Graduate,* Benjamin's; in *Catch-22,* Yossarian's; in *Carnal Knowledge,* Jonathan's; in *The Day of the Dolphin,* Terrell's; and in *The Fortune,* Oscar and Nicky's. The point of view in "Family," however, seems to vary, depending on the episode, perhaps because Nichols does not exercise close directional control.

Nichols and his films are significant in the development of the motion picture in several ways. First of all, he has opened up the way for many subjects that were previously taboo on the screen. With *Who's Afraid of Virginia Woolf?* and *Carnal Knowledge* (and the court cases about them) and to a lesser extent with *The Graduate, Catch-22, The Fortune,* and *The Day of the Dolphin,* Nichols revealed a whole range of subjects that could be treated on the screen. Often these subjects were sexual in nature. He handled them artistically, and all of the symbols were related to the "spines" of his films. Other filmmakers then followed Nichols' lead in dealing, some artistically and some not, with a whole range of subjects that are meaningful to contemporary audiences.

Next, with his excellent taste in casting his films and his outstanding work with actors and actresses, Nichols has started, and/or helped, many actors and actresses to achieve stardom and brilliant careers. Dustin Hoffman, Jack Nicholson, and Katharine Ross are most notable. Many seasoned professionals enjoy working with Nichols, including Alan Arkin, Warren Beatty, Candice Bergen, Richard Burton, William Daniels, Ann-Margret, George C. Scott, Elizabeth Taylor, Sada Thompson, Trish Vandeveer, Elizabeth Wilson, and many others. Like Ingmar Bergman in Sweden, Nichols also uses many of the same actors, actresses, and crew members over and over in his films.

Next, his films are seen by many more people than most *auteurist* films. *The Graudate* is one of the all-time money-makers, and *Who's Afraid of Virginia Woolf?, Catch-22,* and *Carnal Knowledge* share with it a place in *Variety's* "All Time Rental Champs,"[8] those films that have taken in net film rentals of at least $4,000,000 in the United States and Canada. According to the May 11, 1977 *Variety, The Graduate* made $49,978,000; *Who's Afraid of Virginia Woolf?* made $14,500,000; *Carnal Knowledge* made $12,351,000; and *Catch-22* made $12,250,000. Here is a fine artist, with his own profound and complex personal vision, who is popular at the box office. His films are about and reflect the feelings of a subculture, the middle to upper middle class educated, and this group responds. As Alpert points out, the audience that sees *The Graduate* is primarily not the same audience that sees *The Sound of Music*. It can be concluded from the high rentals, however, that Nichols' films are seen by many more people than just a specific faction of the filmgoing public. He has important things to say about and to not only a subculture, but all of us.

Nichols is an excellent film artist who deals eloquently with the human condition. His films exhibit technical competence, personal style, and coherent, profound meaning. He can be ranked with Ingmar Bergman (who, incidentally, is also concerned with beautiful moments, friendship, sex and love, and a difficult world), Michaelangelo Antonioni, Federico Fellini, and other film artists who have achieved excellent fusions of form and content and who deal with problems and concerns related to the contemporary human condition. As John Ford used the western and Alfred Hitchcock used the thriller to express their visions, Nichols has used a certain period of time (from the twenties on) and a certain subculture (the middle to upper middle class educated American) to express his particular vision. I predict that his films will stand the test of time, for although about a certain subculture, they contain aspects of universality, brilliance, and profundity that separate the large artistic accomplishment from the small.

Nichols values the notion of collaboration in his work. He has said, "I don't *think* when I'm alone. That's why I'm a director. I'm turned on by somebody else. A director works with other people. I don't have to sit in a room alone and plan things. I mean I do, but it comes out of a connection with a group of people."[9]

Nichols may certainly get input from many people (and he surrounds himself with the best artists), but the final decisions, the final putting together, the final controlling vision, are his own.

Nichols' artistic vision seems to be based on an honest look at the grimness and tragedy of the human condition, with a tentative, resolving note of hope and nobility.

Notes and References

Chapter One

1. *Current Biography*, 1961, p. 345.
2. "Playboy Interview: Mike Nichols," *Playboy*, June 1966, p. 63.
3. Ibid.
4. Robert Rice, "A Tilted Insight," *The New Yorker*, April 15, 1961, p. 58.
5. *Playboy*, p. 63.
6. Rice, pp. 70–71.
7. "About the Film Makers," Columbia Pictures press release on *The Fortune*, p. 13.
8. Rice, p. 55.
9. Robert Berkvist, "How Nichols and Rabe Shaped 'Streamers,' " *New York Times*, April 25, 1975, II, 12.
10. Skits mentioned (except "Pirandello") can be heard on *Mike Nichols and Elaine May Retrospect* (Chicago: Phonogram, Inc. [formerly Mercury Records Productions, Inc.] SRM 2–628, 1971). Originally recorded between 1958 and 1962.
11. Columbia Pictures press release on *The Fortune*, p. 13.
12. Joseph Gelmis, *The Film Director as Superstar* (Garden City, N.Y.: Doubleday, 1970), p. 282.
13. *Playboy*, p. 73.
14. Jan Dawson, "The Graduate," *Sight and Sound* (Summer, 1968). Reprinted in Joy Gould Boyum and Adrienne Scott, *Film as Film* (Boston: Allyn and Bacon, 1971), p. 191.

Chapter Two

1. Edward Albee, *Who's Afraid of Virginia Woolf?* (New York: Pocket Books, 1971), pp. 3, 89, 195.
2. Joseph Gelmis, *The Film Director as Superstar* (Garden City: Doubleday, 1970), p. 277.
3. Ibid., p. 279.
4. Ibid., p. 275.

161

5. Ibid., p. 278.

6. Malcolm Boyd, "Purgatorial," *Christian Century*, July 27, 1966, p. 937.

7. Gelmis, p. 282.

8. Only rarely is a picture filmed in black and white today because of eventual color television exhibition.

9. Thomas Thompson, "Raw Dialogue Challenges All the Censors," *Life*, June 10, 1966, p. 92.

10. Ibid.

. 11. Vincent Canby, " 'Virginia Woolf' Given Code Seal," *New York Times*, June 11, 1966, p. 21.

12. Thompson, *Life*, June 10, 1966, p. 96.

13. "Censors, Censors Everywhere," *New York Times*, July 3, 1966, II, 1.

14. "Who's Afraid of Virginia Woolf?," *America*, August 6, 1966, p. 142.

15. "Who's Afraid . . . ," *Newsweek*, July 4, 1966, p. 84.

16. Gelmis, p. 277.

17. See Robert Graham Kemper, "Allegory of the American Dream," *Christian Century*, Oct. 5, 1976, p. 1214.

18. Ibid.

Chapter Three

1. Joseph Gelmis, *The Film Director as Superstar* (Garden City, N.Y.: Doubleday, 1970), p. 284.

2. Gelmis, p. 283.

3. "Graduating with Honors," *New York Times*, Dec. 31, 1967, p. 14.

4. For a complete discussion of these comic structures see Gerald Mast, "Comic Structures," in *Film Theory and Criticism*, ed. by Gerald Mast and Marshall Cohen (New York: Oxford University Press, 1974), pp. 458–468.

5. "Cum Laude," *New Republic*, Dec. 23, 1967, p. 22.

6. "A Film for the Great Lost Generation," *The* [London] *Times*, Aug. 8, 1968, p. 9.

7. " 'The Graduate' Makes Out," *Saturday Review*, July 6, 1968, p. 15.

8. Charles Webb, *The Graduate* (New York: The New American Library, Inc., 1963), p. 158.

9. " 'The Graduate' Makes Out," p. 82.

Chapter Four

1. McCandlish Phillips, "Heller Pleased with 'Catch-22' Film," *New York Times*, June 19, 1970, p. 24.

2. Joseph Gelmis, *The Film Director as Superstar* (Garden City, N.Y.: Doubleday, 1970), p. 268.

3. Chuck Thegze, "I See Everything Twice," *Film Quarterly (Fall*, 1970), p. 12.

4. Ibid., p. 13.

5. Ibid., p. 14.

6. Ibid.

7. McCandlish Phillips reports that Joseph Heller was very pleased with Nichols' translation of his book, *New York Times*, June 19, 1970, p. 24.

8. Thegze, p. 10.

9. *A Short History of the Movies* (2nd ed.; Indianapolis: Bobbs-Merrill, 1976), pp. 481–483.

10. Phillips, p. 24.

Chapter Five

1. Herb A. Lightman, "On Location with 'Carnal Knowledge,' " *American Cinematographer*, 52, i (Jan., 1971), p. 37.

2. Ibid., p. 35.

3. Ibid., p. 36.

4. Joan Mellen, *Women and Their Sexuality in the New Film* (New York: Dell, 1973), p. 63.

5. Paul D. Zimmerman, "Love in a Blind Alley," *Newsweek*, July 5, 1971, p. 71.

6. Larry DuBois, "An Interview with Jules Feiffer," *Playboy*, September, 1971, pp. 82–84.

7. Ibid.

8. Stefan Kanfer, *Time*, July 5, 1971, p. 66.

9. Ernest Becker, *The Denial of Death* (New York: Free Press, 1973), p. 169.

10. John Lindsay Brown, "Pictures of Innocence," *Sight and Sound*, 41, ii (Spring, 1972), 102.

11. Joseph Gelmis, *The Film Director as Superstar* (Garden City, N.Y.: Doubleday, 1970), p. 279.

12. Stanley Kauffman, "Carnal Knowledge," *New Republic*, August 21, 1971, p. 35; August 28, 1971, p. 35.

13. For example see Larry Michie, "Supreme Court Thickens Fog Over Obscenity," *Variety*, January 8, 1975, pp. 7, 65.

Chapter Six

1. For an excellent analysis of Rourke see Stanley Edgar Hyman, *The Armed Vision* (New York: Vintage, 1961), 114–131.

2. Nora E. Taylor, "Mike Nichols' Latest: Filming with Dolphins," *Christian Science Monitor*, December 27, 1973, p. B5.

3. Ibid.

4. Vincent Canby, "Film: Underwater Talkie," *New York Times*, December 20, 1973, p. 57.

5. Peter S. Feibleman, "Mike Nichols Tries to Make a Talkie with Dolphins," *Atlantic*, January 1974, p. 81.

Chapter Seven

1. *"The Fortune*—About the Motion Picture," Columbia Pictures press release, p. 2.

2. Frank Rich, "The Misfortune of Mike Nichols: Notes on the Making of a Bad Film," *New Times,* July 11, 1975, p. 59.

3. Ibid., p. 61.

4. Andrew Sarris, *Confessions of a Cultist: On the Cinema, 1955-69.* (New York: Simon and Schuster, 1970), p. 327.

5. Mel Gussow, "Nichols, Fortune Made, Looks to the Future," *The New York Times,* June 3, 1975, p. 26.

6. Rich, p. 59.

7. "The Fortune," *The New Republic,* June 5 and 12, 1975, p. 22.

8. Paul D. Zimmerman, "Madcap Murder," *Newsweek,* May 26, 1975, p. 84.

9. Gussow, p. 26.

10. Vincent Canby, "Nichols' Fortune is Old-Time Farce," *New York Times,* May 21, 1975, p. 49.

11. Gussow, p. 26.

Chapter Eight

1. "Treacherous Tightrope Between Soap and Art," [New Orleans] *Times-Picayune TV Focus,* October 17, 1976, p. 6.

2. *Hollywood Reporter,* August 3, 1977, p. 2.

Chapter Nine

1. Mel Gussow, "Nichols, Fortune Made, Looks to the Future," *New York Times,* June 3, 1975, p. 26.

2. Frank Rich, "The Misfortune of Mike Nichols: Notes on the Making of a Bad Film," *New York Times,* July 11, 1975, p. 61.

3. Peter Wollen, *Signs and Meaning in the Cinema* (Bloomington, Ind.: Indiana University Press, 1972), p. 80.

4. Joseph Gelmis, *The Film Director as Superstar* (Garden City, N.Y.: Doubleday, 1970), pp. 274–275.

5. Ibid., pp. 288–289.

6. Rich, p. 61.

7. "Playboy Interview: Mike Nichols," *Playboy,* June, 1966, p. 70.

8. "All Time Rental Champs," *Variety,* May 11, 1977, pp. 8, 28, 70.

9. Gelmis, p. 291.

Selected Bibliography

Books

ALBEE, EDWARD. *Who's Afraid of Virginia Woolf?* New York: Pocket Books, 1971. The play script that the screenplay was based on.

FEIFFER, JULES. *Carnal Knowledge*. New York: Farrar, Straus and Giroux, 1971. The screenplay, with stills from the film.

GELMIS, JOSEPH. *The Film Director as Superstar*. New York: Doubleday, 1971. A very useful book of interviews, containing an extensive interview with Nichols in a section called "Independents with Muscle."

HELLER, JOSEPH. *Catch-22*. New York: Dell, 1955. The novel that the screenplay was based on.

KILEY, FREDERICK, and WALTER MCDONALD (eds.). *A 'Catch-22' Casebook*. New York: Thomas Y. Crowell, 1973. Contains book reviews, criticism, and an interview with Joseph Heller, plus a large section on the film. Includes Heller on translating the novel into the film, several film reviews and criticism, and even a movie satire comic strip from *Mad*," "Catch-All-22." An outstanding collection.

MELLEN, JOAN. *Women and Their Sexuality in the New Film*. New York: Dell, 1973. This in-depth analysis of how women are portrayed in primarily contemporary films includes an analysis of *Carnal Knowledge*.

MERLE, ROBERT. *The Day of the Dolphin*. Greenwich, Conn.: Fawcett Crest, 1970. The original novel on which the screenplay was based.

SARRIS, ANDREW. *Confessions of a Cultist, 1955–69*. New York: Simon and Schuster, 1970. Reviews by Sarris from *The Village Voice*, including not very favorable pieces on *Who's Afraid of Virginia Woolf?* and *The Graduate*.

WEBB, CHARLES. *The Graduate*. New York: The New American Library, 1963. The original novel on which the screenplay was based.

WOLLEN, PETER. *Signs and Meaning in the Cinema*. Bloomington: Indiana University Press, 1972. Not on Nichols, but a fine presentation of the auteur theory.

165

Periodicals

(Many of the items listed are simply short news notes about Nichols' activities and his films. Only substantial criticisms are annotated.)

"All Time Rental Champs," *Variety*, May 11, 1977, pp. 8, 28, 40, 62, 70, 71.

ALPERT, HOLLIS. " 'The Graduate' Makes Out," *Saturday Review*, July 6, 1968, pp. 14–15, 32. Thoughtful, favorable review of *The Graduate* and how the film relates to its audience.

BART, PETER. "Mike Nichols, Moviemaniac," *New York Times*, July 1, 1967, II, 2. Article about Nichols before he did *The Graduate*.

BERKVIST, ROBERT. "How Nichols and Rabe Shaped 'Streamers,' " *New York Times*, April 25, 1975, II, 1, 12. Good article about Nichols' work with the play.

BOYD, MALCOLM. "Purgatorial," *Christian Century*, July 27, 1966, pp. 937–38. Good review of *Who's Afraid of Virginia Woolf?*, in which Boyd asks the question, "Who's afraid to go on without any of the old props?"

BROWN, JOHN LINDSEY. "Pictures of Innocence," *Sight and Sound*, 41, ii (Spring 1972), 101–103. Discusses the characteristics of Nichols' film work as a whole. He has excellent insights and makes good connections among Nichols' first four films.

CANBY, VINCENT. "The Cold Loneliness of It All," *New York Times*, January 23, 1966, II, 7. Canby's subjective feelings after an interview with Nichols.

———. "Film: Underwater Talkie," *New York Times*, December 20, 1973, p. 57. Reviews the pros and cons of *The Day of the Dolphin*.

———. "I was Sorry to See It End," *New York Times*, July 4, 1971, II, 1, 4. Favorable review of *Carnal Knowledge*, "a political and social history of this country during the last 30 years, as defined, exclusively, in the sexual triumphs, adjustments and disasters of two middle class American nebbishes."

———. "Nichols' *Fortune* is Old Time Farce," *New York Times*, May 21, 1975, p. 49. A favorable review of *The Fortune* as farce.

———. "Public Not Afraid of Big Bad 'Woolf,' " *New York Times*, June 25, 1966, p. 21.

———. "A Triumphant 'Catch,' " *New York Times*, June 28, 1970, pp. 1, 18. A thoughtful and complimentary review of *Catch-22*.

———. " 'Virginia Woolf' Given Code Seal," *New York Times*, June 11, 1966, p.21.

COMBS, RICHARD. "*The Day of the Dolphin.*" *Sight and Sound*, 43, ii (Spring 1974), 117–18. Insightful analysis of the strengths and limitations of the film.

CROWTHER, BOSLEY. "Censors, Censors Everywhere," *New York Times*,

July 3, 1966, II, 1, 12. Crowther relates *Who's Afraid of Virginia Woolf?* to his thoughts on censorship of films in many countries.

———. "Graduating with Honors," *New York Times,* December 31, 1967, II, 1–14. Compares *The Graduate* with the work of Preston Sturges in a rewarding review.

CUTHBERT, DAVID. "Treacherous Tightrope Between Soap and Art," *New Orleans Times-Picayune,* "TV Focus," October 17, 1976, p. 6. This "TV Focus" section is devoted to *Family* and contains many worthwhile articles about the series.

FARBER, STEPHEN. "A Film That Forgets Sex Can Be Fun," *New York Times,* August 1, 1971, II, 9. Discusses *Carnal Knowledge* in terms of content and Nichols' "spare visual style."

FARBER, STEPHEN, and ESTELLE CHANGAS. "*The Graduate,*" *Film Quarterly,* 21, iii, (Spring 1968), 37–41. Excellent analysis of *The Graduate.* The authors discuss Nichols' intention and his accomplishment.

FEIBLEMAN, PETER S. "Mike Nichols Tries to Make a Talkie with Dolphins," *Atlantic,* January 1974, 71–81. A long, very informative article about goings on during the filming of *The Day of the Dolphin.* Feibleman visits the island where Nichols is directing the film.

FRANKS, LUCINDA. "Nichols Puts on a Show Starring His Arabian Horses," *New York Times,* April 26, 1976, pp. 29, 55.

GRANT, HANK. "Rambling Reporter," *Hollywood Reporter,* August 3, 1977, p. 2. A note about Nichols' and the film version of *Annie.*

GROSSMAN, EDWARD. "Bloody Popcorn," *Harper's,* December 1970, 32–40. A thoughtful analysis of the film *Catch-22* and its relationship to other films about war.

GUSSOW, MEL. "Mike Nichols for the Fun of It," *New York Times,* November 26, 1976, pp. C1, C4. Good insights on Nichols' views of comedy in relation to the play "Comedians."

———. "Nichols, Fortune Made, Looks to the Future," *New York Times,* June 3, 1975, p. 26. Relevant quotation from Nichols on *The Fortune* and his work in the future.

HELLMAN, LILLIAN. "And Now—An Evening with Nichols and Hellman," *New York Times,* August 9, 1970, p. 9. Sensitive and revealing interview with Nichols.

KAEL, PAULINE. "*Carnal Knowledge,*" *New Yorker,* July 3, 1971, 43–44. Unfavorable but very interesting review of *Carnal Knowledge.*

KANFER, STEPHEN. "*Carnal Knowledge,*" *Time,* July 5, 1971, pp. 66–67. Favorable review of *Carnal Knowledge,* which argues that the subtext "carries the chill of fastidious puritanism."

KANON, JOSEPH. "Movies, Big Budget Flicks," *Atlantic,* March 1974, 93–94. Favorable review of *The Day of the Dolphin,* "the kind of movie that extends a director's range. . . ."

KAUFFMAN, STANLEY. "*Carnal Knowledge*," *New Republic*, August 21, 28, 1971, pp. 22–35. Insightful review of *Carnal Knowledge*, and excellent comments about Nichols' style. "Nichols is concentrating more and more on the frame—the held shot—as a source of power."

———. "*Catch-22*," *New Republic*, July 4, 1970, pp. 22–23. Discusses why *Catch-22* did not work, in his opinion.

———. "Cum Laude," *New Republic*, December 23, 1967, pp. 22, 37, 38. Insightful, favorable analysis of Nichols' directing and *The Graduate*, "a milestone in American film history."

———. "*The Fortune*," *New Republic*, June 5, 12, 1975, p. 22. Balanced review of the film which praises Nichols' work with actors.

———. "Funless Games at George and Martha's," *New York Times*, June 24, 1966, p. 28. Thoughtful, favorable review of *Who's Afraid of Virginia Woolf?*

———. "Wooden Nichols and Others," *New Republic*, January 19, 1974, p. 22. An unfavorable review of *The Day of the Dolphin*.

KEMPER, ROBERT GRAHAM. "Allegory of the American Dream," *Christian Century*, October 5, 1976, pp. 4–5. The review of *Who's Afraid of Virginia Woolf?* where Kemper uses as a frame of reference the allegory of the American Dream, with George representing George Washington and the child representing the promise of the American Revolution.

LIGHTMAN, HERB A. "On Location with *Carnal Knowledge*," *American Cinematographer*, January 1971, 34–37, 86–88. Really fine reporting from the set of *Carnal Knowledge*, with Richard Sylbert, Production Designer, and Giuseppe Rutunno, ASC, Director of Photography, providing brilliant insights into the design and cinematography of the film.

MACKLIN, F. A. "Benjamin will Survive . . . ," *Film Heritage*, 4, i (Fall 1968), 1–6. An interview with Charles Webb, author of the novel *The Graduate*, about his feelings on the film version of his novel.

O'CONNOR, JOHN J. "TV's 'Family' Celebration," *New York Times*, April 13, 1976, p. 67. Positive review of *Family* after the first six episodes.

PECHTER, WILLIAM S. "M*A*S*H-22," *Commentary*, 50, iii, (September 1970), p. 25. Unfavorable review of *Catch-22*.

"Playboy Interview: Mike Nichols," *Playboy*, June 1966, 63–74. An outstanding interview with Nichols at the time he directed *Who's Afraid of Virginia Woolf?* Nichols talks about his life and his work.

RICE, ROBERT. "A Tilted Insight." *New Yorker*, April 15, 1961, 47–75. An extremely significant article about Nichols' early life and his work with Elaine May. Rice also discusses several Nichols and May skits.

RICH, FRANK. "The Misfortune of Mike Nichols: Notes on the Making of a Bad Film," *New Times*, July 11, 1975, pp. 58–61. An excellent article about the making of *The Fortune*. Rich, who visited the set, strikes a balance between objective reporting and subjective analysis as he gives his impressions of the film and the director.

"Some Are More Yossarian Than Others," *Time*, June 15, 1970, pp. 66–74. Fine cover-story article with excellent insights into *Catch-22* and Nichols himself.

TAYLOR, JOHN RUSSELL. "A Film for the Great Lost Generation," *London Times*, August 8, 1968, p. 9. Points out similarities between *The Graduate* and Andy Hardy movies. A good analysis from a unique frame of reference.

TAYLOR, NORA E. "Mike Nichols' Latest: Filming with Dolphins," *Christian Science Monitor*, December 27, 1973, B5. Taylor talks with Joseph E. Levine about the making of the film.

THEGZE, CHUCK. "I See Everything Twice," *Film Quarterly*, 24, i (Fall 1970), 7–17. A brilliant analysis of the film *Catch-22*, especially where Thegze compares novel and film.

THOMPSON, THOMAS. "Raw Dialogue Challenges All the Censors," *Life*, June 10, 1966, pp. 87–91. An account of the film *Who's Afraid of Virginia Woolf?* and its censorship problems.

"Virginia Woolf to be Shown as a 'For Adults Only' Film," *New York Times*, May 26, 1966, p. 57.

WALSH, MOIRA. "*Who's Afraid of Virginia Woolf?*", *America*, August 6, 1966, pp. 141–43. Positive, thoughtful review of the film and its relationship to its critics.

"Who's Afraid . . . ," *Newsweek*, July 4, 1966, pp. 84–85. Negative review of the film in which the writer argues, "Albee is using his harrowing heterosexual couples as surrogates for homosexual partners having a vicious, narcissistic, delightedly self-indulgent spat."

ZIMMERMAN, PAUL D. "Love in a Blind Alley," *Newsweek*, July 5, 1971, p. 71. Positive review of *Carnal Knowledge* as "the story of two young men who grow older without growing up. . . ."

———. "Madcap Murder," *Newsweek*, May 26, 1975, p. 84. Insightful but negative review of *The Fortune*.

———. "The Porpoise of Life," *Newsweek*, December 3, 1973, pp. 33–34. Mixed review of *The Day of the Dolphin*.

Other Sources

NICHOLS, MIKE, and ELAINE MAY. *Retrospect* (Chicago: Phonogram, Inc. [formerly Mercury Records Productions, Inc.] SRM-2-628, 1971). Some of the finest and famous Nichols and May skits recorded in stereo. The two-record set includes "Bach to Bach," "Telephone," "Adultery," and many more. There is even a cut of Nichols and May at work.

"*The Fortune*—About the Motion Picture," Columbia Pictures Press Release on *The Fortune*, 1975.

Unpublished Works

SCHUTH, H. WAYNE. *The Image of the College in the American Fiction Film with Emphasis on the Work of Mike Nichols: A Study in Belief Systems.* An unpublished Ph.D. Dissertation, The Ohio State University, 1972. Approximately thirty important American fiction films dealing with the issues of higher education are examined. The value systems of the students as related to the value systems of the college authorities and institutions are analyzed, and the relationship between the individual and that large complex of pressures that may loosely be termed authority is explored. Four Mike Nichols films were analyzed in-depth.

Filmography

WHO'S AFRAID OF VIRGINIA WOOLF? (Warner Brothers, 1966)
Producer: Ernest Lehman
Assistant to the Producer: Hal Polaire
Assistant Director: Bud Grace
Production Assistant: Doane Harrison
Screenplay: Ernest Lehman, based on the play of the same name by Edward Albee (1962)
Director of Photography: Haskell Wexler
Production Designer: Richard Sylbert
Editor: Sam O'Steen
Music: Alex North
Costumes: Irene Sharaff
Sound: M. A. Merrick
Set Decorator: George James Hopkins
Script Supervisor: Meta Rebner
Cast: Elizabeth Taylor (Martha), Richard Burton (George), George Segal (Nick), Sandy Dennis (Honey)
Running Time: 129 minutes
Premiere: Criterion and Tower East Theatres on June 24, 1966, New York
16 mm Rental: Warner Brothers Film Gallery

THE GRADUATE (Avco Embassy, 1967)
Producer: Lawrence Turman
Production Supervisor: George Justin
Assistant Director: Don Kranze
Screenplay: Calder Willingham and Buck Henry, based on the novel of the same name by Charles Webb (1963)
Director of Photography: Robert Surtees
Production Designer: Richard Sylbert
Editor: Sam O'Steen
Set Decorator: George Nelson
Assistant Editor: Bob Wyman
Sound: Jack Solomon

171

Script Supervisor: Meta Rebner
Costumes: Patricia Zipprodt
Songs: Paul Simon (sung by Simon and Garfunkle)
Additional Music: Dave Grusin
Panavision
Color by Technicolor
Cast: Anne Bancroft (Mrs. Robinson), Dustin Hoffman (Benjamin Braddock), Katharine Ross (Elaine Robinson), William Daniels (Mr. Braddock), Elizabeth Wilson (Mrs. Braddock), Buck Henry (Room Clerk), Brian Avery (Carl Smith)
Running Time: 105 minutes
Premiere: December 21, 1967, Lincoln Art and Coronet Theatres, New York
16 mm Rental: Audio-Brandon, and other national rental firms

CATCH-22 (Paramount, 1970)
Producers: John Calley and Martin Ransohoff
Unit Production Manager: Joe L. Cramer
Assistant Director: Edward A. Teets
Associate Producer: Clive Reed
Production Manager: Jack Corrick
Second Unit Direction: Andrew Marton, John Jordan, and Alan McCabe
Screenplay: Buck Henry, based on the novel of the same name by Joseph Heller (1955)
Production Designer: Richard Sylbert
Director of Photography: David Watkin
Editor: Sam O'Steen
Art Direction: Harold Michelson
Set Decorator: Ray Moyer
Costume and Hair Supervision: Ernest Adler
Script Supervisor: Meta Rebner
Special Effects: Lee Vasque
Technical Advisor: Major Alexander Gerry
Special Photographic Effects: Albert Whitlock
Title Layout: Wayne Fitzgerald
Rome Production Coordinator: Baccio Bandini
Panavision
Color by Technicolor
Cast: Alan Arkin (Yossarian), Martin Balsam (Colonel Cathcart), Richard Benjamin (Major Danby), Arthur Garfunkel (Nately), Jack Gilford (Doc Daneeka), Buck Henry (Colonel Korn), Bob Newhart (Major Major), Anthony Perkins (Chaplain Tappmann), Paula Prentiss (Nurse Duckett), Martin Sheen (Dobbs), Jon Voight (Milo Minderbinder), Orson Welles (General Dreedle), Bob Balaban (Orr), Susanne Benton (Dree-

dle's Wac), Norman Fell (Sergeant Towser), Charles Grodin (Aarfy
  Aardvark), Jon Korkes (Snowden), Austin Pendleton (Moodus)
"Also Sprach Zarathustra" conducted by Fritz Reiner
Premiere: Paramount and Sutton Theatres, June 24, 1970, New York
Running Time: 121 minutes
16 mm Rental: Films, Inc.

CARNAL KNOWLEDGE (Avco Embassy, 1971)
Producer: Mike Nichols
Executive Producer: Joseph E. Levine
Associate Producer: Clive Reed
Screenplay: Jules Feiffer
Assistant Director: Tim Zinnemann
Director of Photography: Giuseppe Rotunno
Editor: Sam O'Steen
Production Designer: Richard Sylbert
Costumes: Anthea Sylbert
Art Director: Robert Luthardt
Set Decorator: George R. Nelson
Sound: Lawrence O. Jost
Panavision
Color by Technicolor
Cast: Jack Nicholson (Jonathan), Arthur Garfunkel (Sandy), Candice Bergen
  (Susan), Ann-Margret (Bobbie), Rita Moreno (Louise), Cynthia O'Neal
  (Cindy), Carol Kane (Jennifer)
Running Time: 100 minutes
Premiere: June 30, 1971, Cinema I Theatre, New York
16 mm Rental: Audio-Brandon

THE DAY OF THE DOLPHIN (Avco Embassy, 1973)
Producer: Robert E. Relyea
Executive Producer: Joseph E. Levine
Screenplay: Buck Henry, based on the novel of the same name by Robert
  Merle (1967)
Music: George Delerue
Director of Photography: William A. Fraker
Editor: Sam O'Steen
Production Designer: Richard Sylbert
Costumes: Anthea Sylbert
Second Unit Director: Alan McCabe
Set Decorator: George A. Nelson
Sound: Lawrence O. Jost
Panavision
Color by Technicolor

Cast: George C. Scott (Dr. Jake Terrell), Trish Vandeveer (Maggie Terrell),
    Paul Sorvino (Mahoney), Fritz Weaver (Harold DeMilo), Jon Korkes
    (David), Edward Herrmann (Mike), Leslie Charleson (Maryanne),
    John David Carson (Larry), John Denper (Wallingford), Severn Dar-
    den (Schwinn), William Roerick (Dunhill), Elizabeth Wilson (Mrs.
    Rome)
Running time: 104 minutes
Premiere: December 19, 1973, Ziegfield Theatre, New York
16 mm Rental: Swank

THE FORTUNE (Columbia Pictures, 1975)
Producers: Mike Nichols and Don Devlin
Executive Producer: Hank Moonjean
Associate Producer: Robert E. Schultz
Assistant Director: Peter Bogart
2nd Assistant Director: Jerry Grandey
Screenplay: Adrien Joyce
Director of Photography: John A. Alonzo
Music: David Shire
Editor: Stu Linder
Assistant Editor: Arthur R. Schmidt
Production Designer: Richard Sylbert
Costumes: Anthea Sylbert
Production Services: Diamond Service Company
Set Decorator: George Gaines
Art Director: W. Stewart Campbell
Script Supervisor: Annabel Davis-Goff
Production Coordinator: Richard Liebegott
Unit Production Manager: Howard Roessel
Panavision
Color by Technicolor
Cast: Jack Nicholson (Oscar), Warren Beatty (Nicky), Stockard Channing
    (Freddie), Florence Stanley (Mrs. Gould), Richard B. Shull (Chief
    Detective), Tom Newman (John the Barber)
Running Time: 86 minutes
Premiere: Coronet, May 20, 1975, New York
16 mm Rental: Swank

Index

Actor's Studio, 20
Albee, Edward, 27, 31, 34, 38, 39, 41, 42
Alfie, 40
Allen, Jay Presson, 145
American Broadcasting Company, 145, 148
American Dream, The (Albee), 42
Ann-Margret, 91, 159
Antonioni, Michaelangelo, 99, 158, 160
Arabian horses, 20
Arkin, Alan, 21, 159
Avco Embassy Pictures, 85, 126
Auteur theory, 151

Bancroft, Anne, 45
Baxter-Birney, Meredith, 146
Beatty, Warren, 129, 159
Bergen, Candice, 85
Bergman, Ingmar, 159, 160
Berman, Shelley, 21
Billy Jack, 112
Blue Angel, The, 21
Brief Encounter, 23
Broderick, James, 146
Burton, Richard, 23, 27, 37, 38, 159

Cabaret, 145
Censorship, 38–40, 108, 159, 163
Channing, Stockard, 129, 138, 140
Chaplin, Charles, 131
Chekhov, Anton, 111
Cherry Lane School, 19
Chicago, University of, 20, 22
Chinatown, 141

Compass Theatre, 21
Crothers, Scatman, 136

Dalio, Marcel, 75
Dalton School, 19
Daniels, William, 159
Darling, 40
Dennis, Sandy, 27, 38
Disney, Walt, 33
Dr. Dolittle, 124
Drowning (symbolic), 34, 35, 45, 47, 51, 55, 72, 88, 91, 97, 125, 135, 141, 148, 152–53

8½, 40, 79
Erman, John, 145
Evans, Bob, 148
Exorcist, The, 151

"Fabulous Fifties," 21
Farce, 134, 140
Feiffer, Jules, 23, 24, 85, 93, 99, 100, 102–103
Fellini, Federico, 76, 79, 160
Films for television, 145–146
Five Easy Pieces, 129
Ford, John, 160
Frank, Gary, 146
Friendship, 155–57

Garfunkle, Arthur, 46, 85
German Social Democrat Party, 19
Getting Straight, 60
Goldberg, Leonard, 145
Grand Illusion, 75

Green Berets, The, 79

Harris, Barbara, 21
Hartford-Davis, Robert, 145
Hirson, Roger O., 21
Heller, Joseph, 65, 69, 77, 80
Hellman, Lillian, 45
Henry, Buck, 66, 78, 111, 121
Hiroshima, Mon Amour, 79
Hitchcock, Alfred, 37, 160
Hitler, Adolf, 19
Hoffman, Dustin, 45, 159
How I Won The War, 79

Icarus Productions, 152
Icarus myth, 152–153
Importance of Being Ernest, The, 22
"Jack Paar Show, The," 21

Jax Beer, 21
Jordon, Glenn, 145
Joyce, Adrien, 129

Kinon, Richard, 145

La Dolce Vita, 40
Lachmann, Hedwig, 19
Lampert, Zorah, 21
Landauer, Brigitte, 19
Landauer, Gustav, 19
Lassie, 124
Laurel and Hardy, 132, 136
Lehman, Ernest, 27, 38–39
Lester, Richard, 79
Levine, Joseph E., 126
Lilly, Dr. John C., 126
Little, Thomas F. (Monsignor), 40

May, Elaine, 20–24, 49, 75, 151, 153, 158
M*A*S*H, 79
McKeand, Nigel and Carol Evan, 145
McNichol, Kristy, 146
Merle, Robert, 111
Minotaur, 153

National Catholic Office for Motion Pictures, 40
Newman, Tom, 137
New York University, 19

Nichols, Mike: as auteur, 24, 130, 151, 160; childhood, 19, 151; collaboration, 160; comedy theories, 22, 152; hope in *Who's Afraid of Virginia Woolf?,* 157; improvisational comedian, 20–23; skits with Elaine May, 22–23
FILMS (Director):
Carnal Knowledge, 23, 24, 30, 34, 75, *85–108,* 123, 125, 130, 134, 138, 140, 152–59
Catch-22, 34, *65–80,* 90, 107, 108, 111, 114, 124, 152–59
Day of the Dolphin, The, 35, 75, *111–27,* 130, 134, 138, 152–59
Graduate, The, 23, 27, 30, 34, *45–63,* 72, 75, 79, 80, 85, 87, 88, 95, 101, 104, 107, 108, 111, 124, 130, 131, 132, 134, 139, 140, 152–59, 160
Fortune, The, 35, 75, 86, 89, 125, *129–42,* 152–59
Who's Afraid of Virginia Woolf?, The, 23, *27–42,* 61, 72, 75, 79, 80, 86, 94, 104, 105, 107, 108, 124, 125, 130, 134, 139, 152–59.
PLAYS (Actor):
An Evening with Mike Nichols and Elaine May, 21
Journey to the Day, 21
Miss Julie, 20
St. Joan, 22
PLAYS (Director):
Apple Tree, The, 23
Barefoot in the Park, 23
Comedians, 145
Gin Game, The, 148
Knack, The, 23
Little Foxes, The, 45
Luv, 23
Odd Couple, The, 23
Plaza Suite, 45
Prisoner of Second Avenue, The, 111
Purgatory, 22
Streamers, 22, 145
Uncle Vanya, 111
PLAYS (Producer):
Annie, 148
SKITS (with Elaine May):
·"Adultery," 22
"Bach to Bach," 23
"Little More Gauze, A," 22

"Mother and Son," 22
"Pirandello," 22
"Second Piano Concerto," 23
"Telephone," 22
TELEVISION SERIES (Producer):
"Family," 35, 75, *145–48*, 152–59
Nicholson, Jack, 85, 129, .159
Novel into film: *Catch-22*, 69; *Day of the Dolphin, The*, 117, 124; *Graduate, The*, 61.

"Monitor," 21
Motion Picture Association of America, 39

"Omnibus," 21

Parone, Edward, 145
Patton, 79
Pawnbroker, The, 40
Peschkowsky, Paul, 19
Peter Pan, 112
Petulia, 79
Play into film: *Who's Afraid of Virginia Woolf?*, 31–32
"Playhouse 90," 21
Prime of Miss Jean Brodie, 145
Psycho, 37
Psychoanalysis, 62, 65–66, 70, 78, 139

Red Desert, 99
Renoir, Jean, 75
Resnais, Alain, 79
Riefenstahl, Leni, 76
Rollins, Jack, 21
Ross, Katherine, 45, 159
Rotunno, Giuseppe, 98
Rourke, Constance, 111
Rydell, Mark, 145

Salome, 19
Schisgal, Murray, 23
Scott, George C., 111, 159
Segal, George, 23, 27, 38

Semiology, 24
Shepherd, David, 20–21
Shurlock, Geoffrey, 39
Silencers, The, 40
Simon, Neil, 23, 45, 111
Simon, Paul, 46
Sound of Music, The, 160
Spelling, Aaron, 145
Spine (in Nichols' work), 23–24, 32, 34, 35, 37, 38, 63, 66, 99, 159
Stanley, Florence, 132
"Starsky and Hutch," 145
"Steve Allen Show, The," 21
Strasberg, Lee, 20
Strauss, Richard, 19, 73
Strawberry Statement, The, 60
Subber, Saint, 23
Subjective camera, 35, 50, 71
Sullivan, Patrick, J. (Father), 40
Surtees, Robert, 58
"SWAT," 145
Sylbert, Richard, 98, 99

Taylor, Elizabeth, 23, 27, 37, 38, 159
Thompson, Sada, 146, 159
Three Little Pigs, The, 33
Todd, Albert, 111
Turman, Lawrence, 27
Two Tars, 136
2001, 73, 79

Valenti, Jack J., 39
Vandeveer, Trish, 159
Village Voice, The, 85

Watergate, 125
Walden High School, 19
Warner, Jack L., 39
West Side Story, 24
Wilson, Elizabeth, 159
Woolf, Virginia, 33, 42

Zoo Story, The (Albee), 41